W9-CKR-669
1907

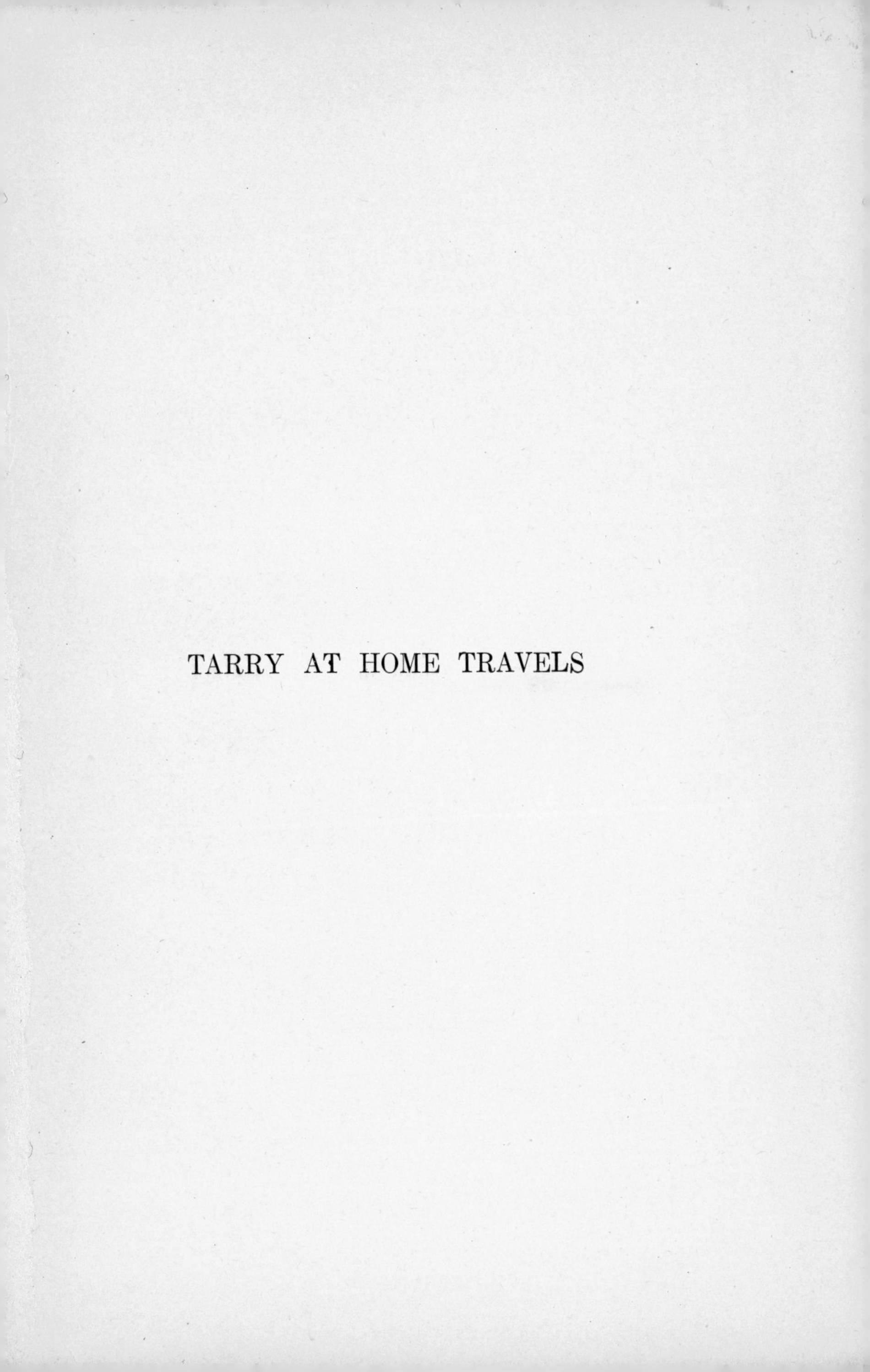

TARRY AT HOME TRAVELS

EDWARD EVERETT HALE.

From a recent photograph by C. M. Bell, Washington.

TARRY AT HOME TRAVELS

BY

EDWARD EVERETT HALE

AUTHOR OF "THE MAN WITHOUT A COUNTRY," "MEMORIES OF A HUNDRED YEARS," ETC.

ILLUSTRATED

"My mind impels me to write on places where I have been and on some of the people whom I have seen in them."

New York
THE MACMILLAN COMPANY
LONDON: MACMILLAN & CO., LTD.
1907

Set up and electrotyped. Published October, 1906.
Reprinted January, 1907.

Norwood Press
J. S. Cushing & Co. — Berwick & Smith Co.
Norwood, Mass., U.S.A.

PREFACE

The papers which make up this book were printed in *The Outlook* with the same title. The first gives the plan and purpose which was substantially held to through the series.

As we now collect them, we are able frequently to add in detail suggestions which have been made by courteous correspondents, — for whose kindness I thank them heartily.

It seemed desirable at the end of the series of travel proper to include two papers on the City of Washington, which had also been printed in *The Outlook*.

EDWARD E. HALE.

Matunuck, Rhode Island,
July, 1906.

CONTENTS

LIST OF ILLUSTRATIONS

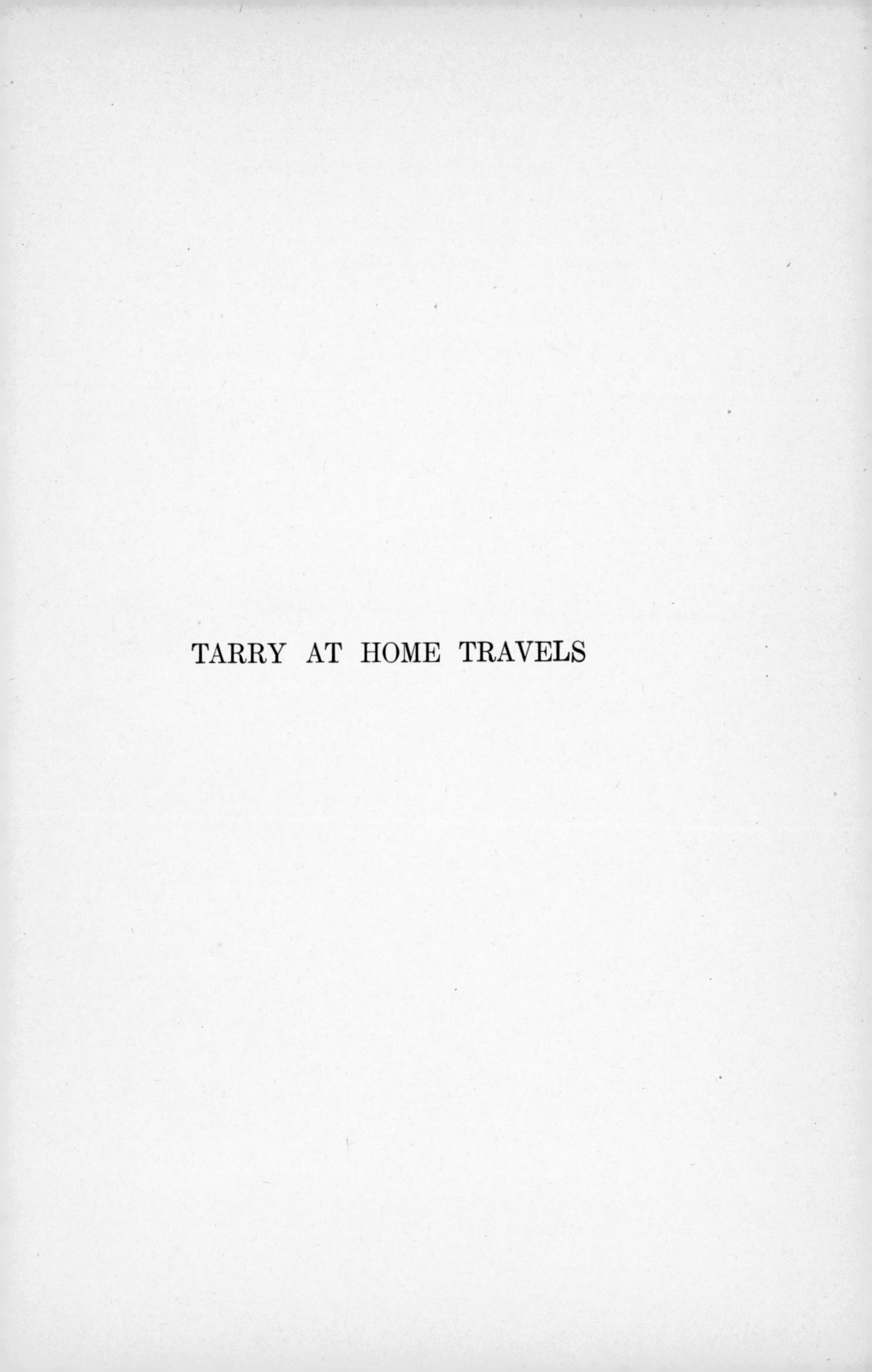

TARRY AT HOME TRAVELS

TARRY AT HOME TRAVELS

CHAPTER I

INTRODUCTORY

It seems to me curious that so few people write about travels in the United States. One in a thousand of the intelligent Americans who travel in Europe puts his observations in print. One in fifty of the people who cross Asia does the same; and every one who crosses Africa does. But of the travellers of America you might count on the fingers of two hands all who have written anything worth reading that has been printed in the last twenty years.

Of which one consequence is that when you talk with intelligent Americans you find that they know more of Switzerland and perhaps of Moscow or of Stonehenge than they know of Indianapolis, or of Trenton Falls, or of Bonaventure, or Chimborazo. You can go to an illustrated lecture and come home and feel afterwards that you have been on a Norwegian canal or a Portuguese railway. But if there are such shows of my own country, I am not favored. I am always on the lookout for them, but I never find them.

A little boy who was a friend of mine was studying arithmetic at school, and he came to the process known by the schoolmasters as "long division." It said in the book, "Inquire how many times the Divisor goes into the Dividend." So when he had his slate adjusted to Divisor and Dividend, he went to ask his teacher how far one went into the other. She remonstrated, but he said that that was what the book said — it told him to "inquire," and he "inquired."

The average American is left in very much the condition of that boy. If he wants to know about Vermont, he cannot find any book that tells him. Whoever he speaks to about it is annoyed or pretends to gape, and tells him to go to Vermont and see. The newspapers are painfully provincial. It is hard to make them print some spirited letter from a bright friend who is travelling in the steps of Lewis and Clark, or among the wonders of California. Once there were such books as Lewis and Clark's or Frémont's, or Francis Parkman's or Dwight's "Travels in New England," or Flint's "Mississippi." But, as I say, we do not find such books now. One recollects, of course, "The Wedding Journey" of Howells, and "A Chance Acquaintance," and other such fragments. But not enough of them. I sent to a magazine a good story once, where the bride and her husband travelled on the Vanderbilt lines. I had to strike out this allusion lest it should be an advertisement!

I should like to have exactly such a book about the United States as an English doctor, whose name I have forgotten, made about the continent of Europe just after Napoleon was sent to Elba. English people had been shut off from the continent for half a generation. In fact, unless they were named Arthur Young, Addison, or Prior, or Sterne, or John Milton, they had not gone there much before. One of the charms of Jane Austen's novels is that they are exquisitely insular. A post-captain or an admiral may be alluded to because Britannia rules the waves. But the continent of Europe or the double continent of America is referred to no more than the Planet Neptune, of which she had never heard. This unknown English doctor sent his English carriage across to Calais, made up a party of four, took his life in his hands, and rode to Italy and back again, and told from day to day just what he had seen. It is graceless of me to forget his name, for he wrote a very entertaining book. Dear old Dr. Dwight, the President of Yale College, started from New Haven, a hundred years ago, and jumbled about the New England states and wrote an account of them in just the same way. Our friend Mr. Lummis started with his dog, both on foot, from Chillicothe in Ohio and walked to Los Angeles in California. The dog died, but Mr. Lummis wrote a very entertaining book about the journey. But Dr. Dwight is in heaven; I suppose the English doctor is, for if he were alive, he

EASTPORT AND PASSAMAQUODDY BAY.
From a print published in London in 1839.

must be one hundred and thirteen years old; and Mr. Lummis is too busy with his magazine to start again. So I am writing these lines, not so much for what they tell as to call the attention of readers to what they do not tell. Think of the great voids of ignorance! Think how little you know about North Dakota or Idaho!

Of course modern science answers that we should travel ourselves. We should see with our own eyes and hear with our ears and understand with our hearts the wonderful things which are in our own country, and then should turn round and tell them to others. As Tasso says,

> When I am left to tell in other's ear
> The wonders seen, and whisper, "I was there."

But in face of this scientific course there are difficulties. One, it costs so much to travel in America. I can go about anywhere in Spain or Switzerland, and at the end of the week I only have to draw for twenty-five dollars from my banker. But in America, wherever I go, the railways make me pay so much, and the hotels make me pay so much, and the steamboats, that just as I am ready for my grand tour in America, some one says to me, "Take a second-class ticket with me for Hamburg;" and I do, and we travel in Bohemia instead of going to Tacoma. It is only by pretending to be a schoolmaster and taking a half-price ticket to attend an "Educational Convention" — as if there were any such word as "educational," and as if there were much use in a convention — it is only thus that I can go to see Bunker Hill, if I happen to live in the North Park. All of which we will hope the future will reform for us.

Having said this, I will try to start the intelligent reader on his own feet; and we will give him some hint of what he ought to see, and I will not pretend to show it to him. He shall have some other hint of what he ought to hear, but I will not pretend to speak it. Some of the best essays about this world which have been written are the prefaces to Murray's and Baedeker's Guide Books. They do not tell the traveller what he is to see. That comes afterwards in the book. But they try to quicken his enthusiasm, to make him see that travel is worth while, and to understand that it is neither so dangerous

LORD ASHBURTON.
From a mezzotint by Wagstaff, after the painting by Sir Thomas Lawrence.

nor so difficult as he supposes. I will try here, mostly by memories, sometimes by expectations, with an occasional word of the present fact, to interest the average reader in some plan for seeing some part of his own home, which he has never seen until now.

There are two notable studies of New England which you had better read right through before you make your plans for next June. They are in the first volume and the second of Dr. Palfrey's "History of New England." They not only tell what he knew, which was a great deal, but they give you almost all the references which you need if you have the genuine historical passion. The average American has no such passion. He does not care anything about history. This is indeed the proverb of the hustling editor of to-day — that even newspapers have nothing to do with history. One of them, with pathetic blindness, quoted from Jules Verne the remark that you got no history out of the newspaper, really thinking that Jules Verne intended this for a compliment. But there are occasional people who are curious to know where the plant of Indian corn came from, and what sort of a seed it had; where the pine tree came from, and what sort of a seed it had. And that sort of people like to know what the Thirteen States were, and how they are different from the thirty-two others; what a New England forest was, and how it differs from the New England of factories and high schools; who Massasoit or Canonicus were, and how they differed from Charles William Eliot and John Davis Long. These people are the people who care for history, and they will be glad of such references as Dr. Palfrey gives them; and they will be glad to read the chapters of which I have spoken; and in very rare cases they will go to the American Antiquarian Library or the John Carter Brown collection of books in Providence, or the Massachusetts Historical Society's Library, or to that of Harvard College, or to the Howard Library in New Orleans to see for themselves the original authorities.

For our present purpose it must be enough to say that New England is a peninsula included within an oblong which, if roughly drawn, measures eight degrees of latitude and nine of longitude — a little more accurately, perhaps, sixty or eighty thousand square miles, be the same more or less. Dear Dr. Palfrey says with a certain pride that it is just halfway from the Equator

DANIEL WEBSTER.
From an engraving by H. Wright Smith, after the painting by J. Ames.

to the Pole, and this is interesting, for it gives some slight scientific authority to Dr. Holmes's claim that the gilded dome of the Boston State

House is the "Hub of the Universe." Indeed, it would amuse the first class in the ninth grade of some grammar school to see how nearly that same gilded dome is at the centre of inhabited New England. Possibly some advanced student in that class may find out, what is unknown to all the readers of these lines, why the accomplished architect Charles Bulfinch put a pineapple on top of the dome.

Some of the old writers really thought that New England was an island. What they knew was that Henry Hudson had worked his way in the *Half Moon* up from the ocean on the south as far as Albany; that Champlain had come by water from the ocean on the north as far as Lake Champlain; that between Albany and the head of Lake George there is not a wide distance. In point of fact, I believe the neck of land between the waters which flow into the St. Lawrence and the waters which flow into the Hudson is not more than two miles across. If anybody cares, it was within twenty miles of this neck that Burgoyne received his *coup de grâce*, and that the history of modern civilization changed when, in his capitulation, the independence of the United States was made sure.

I was once at an evening party, talking with

JOHN A. ANDREW.
War Governor of Massachusetts.

one of the great New Englanders, John Albion Andrew, when Louis Agassiz joined us. I said, "Agassiz, I wish you would tell Andrew what I am telling him; you would do it so much better than I." Naturally, he asked me what I was telling him. Now, it was at the time of one of our prehistoric quarrels with England, when the understanding between the two countries was not as cordial as it is now. England and the United States were quarrelling about 54–40, or codfish, or something — I have forgotten what. I said, "I am telling Andrew how you told us that when the Lord God thought he would make a world out of a spinning ball of red-hot water and steam which there was, he made some rocks rise up as a sort of nucleus of the man-habitable world, and that the first thing he thought of was to make the ridge between the United States and Canada."

Agassiz laughed, and said that he had not put it in exactly that way, but that that was the truth. And whoever reads the old treaty of 1783 will be edified in finding that "the highlands between the waters flowing into the St. Lawrence" and the waters flowing into the Atlantic were named by those ungeological diplomatists who made the treaty, as the northern boundary of New England. That critical ridge of rock which poked its head up on that fine morning described in the ninth verse of the first chapter of Genesis may still be traced by the amateur fisherman who has gone up to the narrow trout brook at the head of the Connecticut. It is the same rock which you pass on the Vanderbilt road, just north of the Mohawk, at Little Falls and along in such places, if you are on Howells's "Wedding Journey" or on Lucy Poor's.

Lord Ashburton and Mr. Webster agreed for the northeastern part of the country to make an artificial line. But you and I, for the convenience of things, may recollect that all of us New Englanders probably live above the oldest land in the world. That is the reason of a certain arrogance which other people accuse us of. But, really, we have not much to do with that steaming rock of a hundred million æons ago, for all New England was made over again, it seems, when the glaciers came down from the north, covering us all over with a sheet of ice which was a thousand feet thick, or more, even over the top of our Mount Washington. It drifted

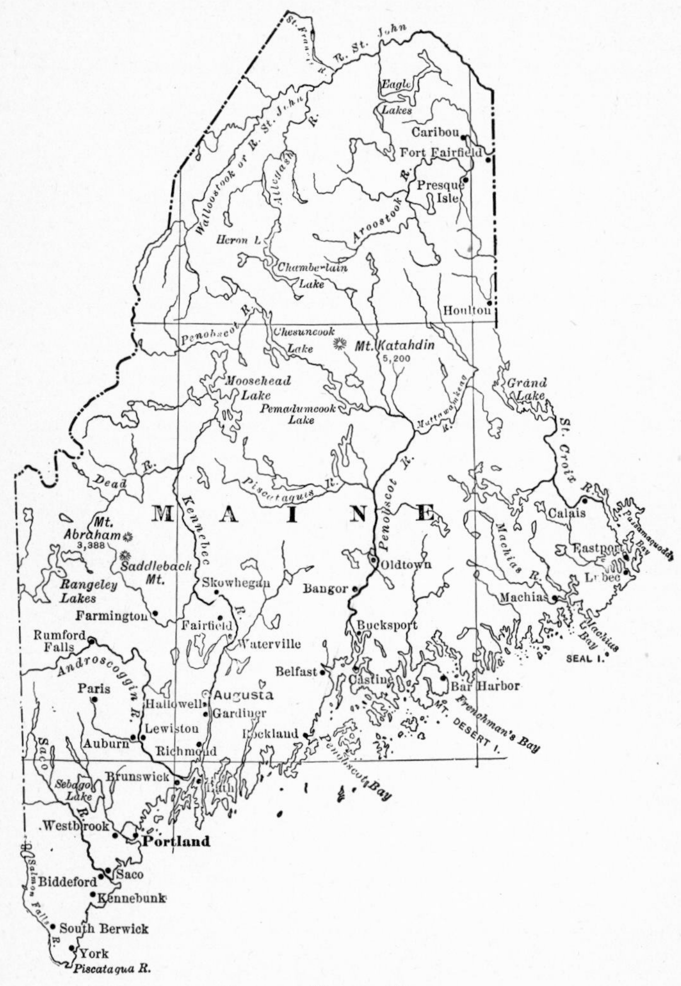

OUTLINE MAP OF MAINE.

south and south and south, until the Atlantic Ocean proved to be too warm for it. It left its gravel and sand and smaller boulders first in a ridge which became Long Island, Block Island, and Nantucket, and, after years more, it made another ridge which is now southern Connecticut and southern Rhode Island and Cape Cod, I suppose, including, among other excellent places, my own summer home. And, still again, it made a third ridge, five or ten miles inland from the Long Island Sound of to-day. Recollect this, my sophomore friend, when walking through New England with your nightgown and toothbrush in a knapsack. Recollect this, Madam Champernoon, as your chauffeur takes you along the Connecticut Valley at a rate not exceeding fifteen miles an hour, as required by the statute, in those last happy moments before the boiler explodes and you and he leave the study of terrestrial geology.

Of this territory, of which we have established the age in such satisfactory and substantial fashion, the state of Maine makes nearly one-half — thirty-three thousand square miles. The people of Maine call it the "*State* of Maine," with a certain pride and frequency not observable in other states. You say Delaware did this or

MOUNT KATAHDIN.

Ohio did that, when a Maine man is a little apt to say, "the State of Maine" did this and the "State of Maine" did that. This is because from near the beginning until 1820 it was the District, or vernacular "Deestrict," of Maine.

Under the passage of what is known as the Missouri Compromise Act in our politics, it was set apart as a state. And the older people still remember with pride that it is no longer the "Deestrict," but it is the state of Maine — a pride which asserts itself even when they are unconscious of what they are saying.

Maine and Vermont are virtually the youngest of the New England states. This is because in practice in the beginning people did not like to go into wildernesses to settle them, although they knew very well what happy homes they would make. They did not like to, while there was any fear of French attack upon the north. The French always brought Indians with them. And you may charge it to the French religion or not as you choose, but the savage warfare which they carried on under French direction was of the most horrible kind. If anybody cares, it is to be observed that the hatred of the Roman Catholic Church which existed formerly in New England was due to the memory that the savage raids of the eighteenth century were in all instances mixed up with French invasion, and were ascribed by the sufferers to the machinations of Latin priests. But with General Wolfe at Quebec in 1759 such French domination practically ended — no more terror of savage warfare. And then New Hampshire people were glad enough to leave their gravel and rock for the fertile valleys of Vermont, and the Massachusetts people glad enough to send their emigrants up into the valleys of the Kennebec and Penobscot. Before that time Maine was simply a fringe of seaboard towns.

NATHAN HALE.
From an old engraving.

My father was a born geographer, and before he died he found, rather to his own surprise, I think, that he was a great engineer. I am apt to think that I and my children inherit from him certain tastes and habits which our nearest friends sometimes venture to call Bohemian.

What I know is that I was born in the month of April, 1822, and that before I was four months old he had taken us all to Dover, New Hampshire, to be noted here as the oldest town in that state. There he left my mother and her four little children in the country tavern of the day while he and the great botanist, Dr. Jacob Bigelow, and two or three friends of theirs went on horseback through the Notch of the White Mountains. Their account of this expedition contains, I think, the first scientific narratives regarding those mountains. They were published at the time in a tract, now rare, which has an interest for us Appalachians.

This expedition was the first bit of travel which ever took me outside of Massachusetts. I do not affect to remember the New Hampshire of that time, but I like to record this adventure. A charming cousin of mine, one of the finest women of the century, used to tell me with amusement that she had made my acquaintance there and then, while I still wore the simpler garments of babyhood. Let this be the prelude to these memories of my own dealings afterwards with the different states of New England.

CHAPTER II

THE STATE OF MAINE

FIRST of Maine. "*Dirigo*, I lead," is the fine motto of that state. Its people have no reason to be ashamed of it or to blush because their fathers chose it. It means, if you are modest, that Maine begins the list of the United States, because in those days men began at the north and repeated the list from north to south. So it was Maine, New Hampshire, Vermont. In these days the Pacific state of Washington runs farther north, to the parallel of 49. But in the days of the district of Maine no state ran so near the North Pole as she did. So Maine does lead for every schoolboy and every schoolgirl of America.

If, again, anybody cares, one of Samuel Hale's grandsons moved out into eastern Maine, while one of his sons moved into Connecticut. The son of this Connecticut man was my grandfather. And he was cousin, if you please, of the grandfather of those men from Maine who now find their companions in Senates and stand unawed before kings. But I did not know that when I first went there. I believe I only mention it now to say that the Hales of Maine are our sort of Hales; the Hales of New Hampshire are of the sort of the distinguished lady I have spoken of, and are also of our kind of Hales, "the Hales who do not have sugar in their coffee." The Hales of Vermont are of the Newbury Hales, which means Thomas the Glover. They also are admirable people, and they have a Nathan Hale of their own who was a Captain Nathan Hale of the Revolution, and died a prisoner of war near New York and shall be spoken of hereafter. My son Philip is an artist. He was in a New York gallery one day when it was what the artists call "varnishing day," and a lady, referring to his picture, said, "So you have come to New York to be hanged, Mr. Hale." "Yes," said he; "that is the way the Hales usually come."

Perhaps it is as well to say that the Massachusetts Hales are some of them of one kind and some of another, and yet a third belong to the

SAMUEL LONGFELLOW.

Rehoboth Hales. The Rhode Island Hales are mostly Rehoboth Hales. Besides the Coventry Hales in Connecticut, of whom I am, and the Ashford Hales, who are our cousins, are the

Glastonbury Hales. They are the people who now produce peaches for the world, and are our cousins on another line from the Ashford Hales.

It is my belief that in all these lines the Hales were cousins of each other. Generally speaking, they are tall, with a tendency to black hair. Without exception they love their country and tell the truth. So much for genealogy, to which I may never refer, perhaps, again.

No, I did not go to Maine to see my cousins. I went there on my way to New Hampshire to see, if you please, on those mountains the geological order of its stratification. In the year 1841 I was appointed as a junior member on the New Hampshire Geological Survey, under the eminent Charles Thomas Jackson, who is better known as one of the discoverers of the properties of ether. On my way to join this survey I went down to Portland and made a visit on my lifelong friend Samuel Longfellow. He is the Longfellow to whom you owe some of the best hymns in your hymn-book; for instance, he wrote the hymn for my ordination. He graduated with me at Cambridge in 1839. And we of our class used to call the celebrated Henry Wadsworth Longfellow the brother of the "Poet Longfellow," meaning that he was brother to our Sam.

Henry Wadsworth Longfellow.

This narrative should really begin with a voyage down Portland Harbor in a boat piloted by Sam Longfellow and me. He and I and Channing, who had asked for my appointment on the New Hampshire Survey, were intimate in college.

From college days down I liked Channing and Channing liked me. In November, 1838, he proposed that we should watch from midnight onward for the annual recurrence of the meteoric shower which is now generally called the shower of the Leonids. And we did so, eight of us of the college class of 1839, on the Delta of those days. What says the poem of that day?

Our Chase and our Channing
The Northwest are scanning,
While the cold wind is fanning
  Their faces upturned,
While our Hurd and our Hale,
With watching turned pale,
Are looking toward Yale
  Where all these things burned.
And Morison and Parker
Cry out to the marker,
"One jet black and darker
  From zenith above."
While Adams and Longfellow,
Watching the throng below,
Won't all night long allow
  Black meteors move.

All the rest of us insisted that there were black meteors as well as white ones. This opinion has been confirmed since then. Our observatory was a square table, just where the statue of John Harvard sits in bronze to-day. North,

JUDGE STEPHEN LONGFELLOW.
Father of Henry Wadsworth and Samuel Longfellow.
From a painting.

south, east, and west of the table were four chairs, facing in those directions, and in them sat four of the club. A fifth, with a lantern on the table, recorded the observations. If any one wants to see them, he can look in *Silliman's Journal* of the next January, or in the Bulletins of the Astronomical Department of the French Academy of Sciences. That was my first appearance on that august record. The little club of observers called itself the Octagon Club. Chase afterwards won distinction as a mathematician. Morison was Provost of the Peabody Library at Baltimore, Adams distinguished himself as a lawyer before his early death, Longfellow was the preacher and hymn-writer, and Parker and Hurd every man's friends. We have never printed till now their "Octagonal Scribblings."

And so in 1841 Channing came into my schoolroom one day and asked me to join him as a subaltern in the Geological Survey of New Hampshire, under Jackson. And, so I did. If this series ever passes Maine, and the reader and I should get into New Hampshire together, I will tell of those experiences. But now, as I have said, Maine is the first on the list, and with Maine we will begin.

To start on this expedition I went to Portland. Then with Longfellow I crossed the southwest corner of Maine, that I might join Channing. In the expedition which followed we ascended Mount Washington, as this reader shall hear when we come to New Hampshire. So, naturally enough, four years after, he proposed to me that we should try the highest mountain in Maine and ascend Mount Katahdin. Before the reader is twenty years older the ascent of Katahdin and the exploration of the Maine lakes will be among the most interesting incidents of familiar summer travel in America.

But of Maine I knew nothing but the Sebago Lake and the Fryeburg road till I went there with this same William Francis Channing for this Katahdin expedition, as my father had gone to New Hampshire to ascend Mount Washington.

I am writing soon after Channing's death, and I am tempted to say that while he is remembered as a distinguished electrician, it is a wonder to some of us that he never became one of the most distinguished men of his time. He was what is now called a physicist of remarkable resources. He had studied with Dr. Robert Hare, who is still remembered among the fathers of science in America, the inventor of the oxyhydrogen blow-pipe. Channing had early taken up the business of harnessing electricity. He is the author of the fire alarm, now in use in all our cities.

> A wizard of such dreaded fame,
> That when, in Salamanca's cave,
> Him listed his magic wand to wave,
> The bells would ring in Notre Dame.

Indeed, in many lines his early experiments in electricity led the way for those who have given to us the electrical inventions of to-day. I count it as a great misfortune for him that as a little boy he was taken to Europe to school. But Fellenberg was a great apostle of education then; his school at Hofwyl, now forgotten, was the Mecca of educators. For those were the days when even sensible people really thought that people could be instructed into the kingdom of heaven, or practically that if you knew your

Bowdoin College in its Early Days.

From an old print.

multiplication table well enough, all else would follow.

Poor little Will Channing, in those early experiences at Hofwyl, lost in childhood the joy and delight, so necessary to the children of God, of easy intercourse with his fellow-men. There was always a certain aloofness about him which made him unhappy. It is not nice to be on the outside margin of any circle of mankind. Here is, for better, for worse, my explanation of the reason why his name does not stand higher than it does among the men of his generation.

I think he and I were the first persons who had ascended Mount Katahdin with scientific tastes and for any scientific purpose. My dear friend Professor Asa Gray had told me that it was desirable to have specimens of the Alpine vegetation there, that it might be compared with that of Mount Washington. I was able to send him more than twenty varieties on my return.

We consulted with Dr. Jackson, who had been our old chief in New Hampshire, and Dr. Jackson had said, in his offhand way, that, passing across

Maine from the coal of Nova Scotia and the limestone of Thomaston, we should come to primitive rock in Mount Katahdin, and that the eastern half of the state of Maine thus presented in very short distances specimens of all the stratifications of the earth's surface from the oldest time to our own. The remark has not much scientific interest, but I have always treasured it as a very good aid to memory as to what Maine is. You can see the beaver build his hut at the north end of Maine, and the next day you can see the Fine Arts Department of Bowdoin College, which is as good a type of the best modern life as you could choose. So you can pass from primitive rock to the latest Tertiary.

Dr. W. O. Crosby, who knows much more about the matter than Dr. Jackson ever pretended to know, says to me, "Between Nova Scotia or Thomaston and Mount Katahdin we have formations covering a wide range of geological time and including some of the oldest as well as the very newest."

If any one is curious about Katahdin, I refer

The Falls of Sault on the Chaudière. On the Route of Arnold's Detachment of 1775.

From "Arnold's Expedition to Quebec," by John Codman, 2d.

him to the magazine *Appalachia* of April, 1901, where I have printed my journal of the time of that ascent. I have said thus much of it by way of inducing readers to make this excursion.

Very simply, the heart of Maine is "the Lake Country" of the eastern United States, precisely as Minnesota is "the Lake Country" of the Mississippi Valley, and as we talk of the Lake Country of England when we go to Windermere. No man knows New England as seen by his own eye who has not sat on the higher summits of Katahdin. In Thoreau's books there will be found an account of his ascent. And, not to occupy more space here, I like to say that the adventure which shall take any man up the Kennebec by such of its head waters as come from the north, so that he thus may strike the route of Arnold's detachment of 1775, makes a very interesting journey. When Mr. Jared Sparks made that journey in his varied historical research, they told him that no traveller had gone through that way since Arnold's men passed by. Or if you will go up to Houlton, which was a military post in the early part of the last century, you will now find a beautiful modern city with the best appliances. Indeed, Aroostook County, of which Houlton is the shire town, is so prosperous a region that they told me when I was last there that there was not an empty house in the county. I know I found schools with the very latest advantages both in Houlton and Fort Fairfield. And yet, as I said just now, beavers are building their dams in the wilderness there.

The Webster-Ashburton Treaty of the year 1842 settled the old boundary controversy between this country and England, which had existed for nearly sixty years. Mr. Webster and Lord Ashburton were the negotiators, but as the territory in question belonged wholly to the states of Maine and Massachusetts, Mr. Webster had present at Washington four commissioners from Maine, three from Massachusetts, and also my father, Nathan Hale, as his personal friend, because my father had given special attention to the boundary question. There were thus ten persons in all who discussed the subject together.

When it was all over, Lord Ashburton told my father that of the ten, he, the English delegate, was the only one who had ever been in the

JAMES BOWDOIN.
After the painting by Gilbert Stuart in the Walker Art Building, Bowdoin College.

territory surrendered. When he was Mr. Baring, he crossed it on a journey between Quebec and Halifax. The route of the New Brunswick and

Canada Railway now passes from the southeast to the northwest through the territory which we conceded to England.

Half-fashionable America knows now how interesting is the region where New England was first settled by the French in 1602. For there is no better central point from which to explore that region than Bar Harbor. And Bar Harbor is very near Dr. Palfrey's sacred parallel of forty-five degrees north. Eastport has some curious history relating to the long period when it was under English government in the War of 1812. It is the only proper American city which has ever been for a long time in the military possession of a foreign power.

But this paper is not written as if it were a guide book. It is rather as if I met you, Gentle Reader, in a palace car as you and Mrs. Reader and the children were speeding eastward from the heats of Baltimore and Philadelphia, and had made up your mind to go as far as you could under the Stars and Stripes. I hope I should not lay out a route for you. I am trying to tell you what are your opportunities in a state which in the continent of Europe would make a very decent empire. Forests and game? Oh, yes. Take the "Flyer" which the Aroostook Railroad people give you, and you will suppose that man was made for nothing but to shoot deer or moose in the wilderness. Or here is another "Flyer" which will tell you about matchless salmon and salmon trout and the rest of the fishy literature. What I want you to understand about Maine is that these people are well poised, well educated, proud, and well satisfied with the place where they are.

It was my duty once to appoint the chief of a new industrial school. Almost of course, I consulted Samuel Chapman Armstrong, "the first citizen of America," who was at the head of the Hampton Institute. He said at once, "Go to Maine, and you are almost sure to find the man you want there." He specified their State College at Orono, but he went farther to say that in Maine they had the fine nobility of New England blood, with the simple habits of the old

New Englander and the New Englander's determination to excel the rest of mankind. President Robbins, of the Waltham Watch Company, once told me that once a year he sent an accomplished lady into the upper valley of the Kennebec, and that she stayed there a month or two enlisting a party of well-educated young women who should come back with her to Waltham in Massachusetts. It is thus, gentle reader, that your Waltham watch is one of a company of a million or two, one of which on one happy day once corrected the standard of Greenwich Observatory.

William DeWitt Hyde, D.D.
President of Bowdoin College since 1885.

I spoke just now of beavers at the north and of the picture gallery in Bowdoin College which is within smell of the ocean on the south. Do not go up to the north to kill beavers, but you may make yourself a "camp" there and stay a fortnight while you watch their sensible enterprises. Or go down to the Commencement at Bowdoin and find yourself in the midst of their traditions of Hawthorne, Longfellow, Andrew, Chandler, Packard, and Upham, or in that fresh present life which Dr. Hyde leads so well.

I loitered there one day to study the crayons and other drawings which the younger Bowdoin brought from Spain and from Italy. I had never seen that collection rivalled excepting one day when Ruskin showed me somewhat similar portfolios in English Oxford, and I cannot help wishing that somebody, even now, would give us a study of the lives of the two Bowdoins, father and son. Here was the Governor of Massachusetts who, under the name of the "President of the Council," "ran Massachusetts" from 1775 till 1780, and afterwards succeeded

Hancock as Governor. Here was his son who was travelling in Europe when Lexington called him home. He was one of our early diplomatists, and he became the benefactor of Bowdoin College. He left his library, his philosophical reports, and his paintings, with six thousand acres of land and the reversion of the island of Naushon, to this College. His mineralogical collection was the nucleus of the cabinets which Professor Cleveland studied and illustrated.

Ah! here is one of my failures to put the right thread into the right needle at the right time. It must be twenty years ago that I was the guest of the College for some function, and had the pleasure of sitting at the Commencement dinner. Dr. Packard was presiding, loved and honored by everybody who knew him. James Gillespie Blaine was at the height of his fame, and admired and loved by everybody in that assembly. And when he was called upon to speak he spoke with all that personal charm which belonged to his speeches when he was talking of that which really interested him. He characterized Dr. Packard to his face, and, to our delight, told us what manner of man he was. With an old reporter's instinct, I seized

PROFESSOR ALPHEUS SPRING PACKARD.
After the painting by F. P. Vinton in the Walker Art Building, Bowdoin College.

the printed menu at my side and began writing on the back the words as they fell from his lips; but in an instant more some Philistine voice said within me: "Why do you do this? There are six reporters at their table eagerly taking it better than you could." And I laid my pencil by. Alas and alas! there was some football match at Princeton or at Harlem that day. The blue pencil of all editorial offices struck out Mr. Blaine's address for the more important details of a touchdown by Smith when Jones had dropped the ball in the gravel, and so that speech was lost. Before the week was over Dr. Packard had died, and I have been left with the wish that on a great occasion I had done what I wanted to do and could do.

Moral. — It is always better to do a thing than not to do it, if you remember duly the Twelve Commandments.

Yes, if there were room to talk of people, there are many, many men who won their laurels in Maine who deserve a place in any Hall of Fame: Champlain, whose monument is his own lake; Baron Castine, whose life is a romance; Knox, who "created all the stores of war" and has left behind him men and women for whom we are all grateful (he went down to Maine and

General Henry Knox.

From the painting by Charles Willson Peale in the Old State House, Philadelphia.

opened up Knox County after his last shotted cannon had been fired at Yorktown); Lincoln, Washington's friend and sometimes his adviser; or, in these later days, Evans, Fessenden, James G. Blaine, and my own chief, Senator Frye, the President to-day of the United States Senate.[1]

There is an excellent story which I can repeat nearly correctly, though I was not on the spot where the speech was made. Our Senator Frye was to address the assembly which met when a stone library building was consecrated, which had been erected to the memory of Mrs. Washburne in Livermore by her sons. Before the address Mr. Frye had been in the old Washburne mansion house. This gave him a chance to say that he had seen that day the cradle in which she had rocked three governors, four members of the House of Representatives, two senators in the United States Senate, two ministers plenipotentiary, one major-general in the army, and one captain in the navy. This is a long catalogue, but if the reader will study

[1] 1904.

the lives of Elihu B. Washburne, of W. B. Washburne, Israel Washburne, and Captain S. W. Washburne, he can fill out the blanks in Mr. Frye's catalogue.

How one would like to show how near these men and other Maine men have been to the centres of our American life! Bowdoin College in her list of alumni counts Hawthorne, Henry Longfellow, Dr. Cleveland, both Hamlins and Packard and the Chandlers, Carroll Everett, and Governor Andrew and so many more. Let me speak of the Greenleafs of Huguenot blood, who came from Newburyport after the war and settled on the upper Penobscot. Of them is Simon Greenleaf, the jurist, and Moses Greenleaf, who made the map of Maine on the wall yonder. His son was my dear and near friend, my other self, may I say? — Frederic William Greenleaf, who died in 1852. I was thirty, and he a year or two older. He is the Harry Wadsworth of my book, "Ten Times One is Ten."

I spoke above of my first visit in Portland. The Longfellow house on Main Street is preserved, one is so glad to say in this age of destruction. When I was first there, Judge Longfellow was still alive. He had served the state to great

THE LONGFELLOW HOUSE IN PORTLAND.

purpose; perhaps he did not know then how his name was going down to the next century. My Samuel Longfellow must have been born in 1819. I saw him first on an August morning in 1835, at about six o'clock in the morning. I had ridden to Cambridge from Boston in what Dr.

Holmes would have called a "one-horse shay," to be examined for admittance at the College. Almost at the moment when we arrived, my brother and I, in front of "University," two more chaises arrived, both of them, as it proved, from the "State of Maine," so simple were the arrangements of those days. In one of them was Francis Brown Hayes, my friend from that hour till he died. In the other was Samuel Longfellow, of whom I may say the same. He was my groomsman when I was married; he wrote the hymn for my ordination. North and south, east and west, we always corresponded with each other. He was one of those, as I have said, who sat where John Harvard now sits, counting the shooting stars. It was he and I who took that voyage of which I have spoken when we counted the islands in Casco Bay. It is queer that I should say this of myself, but it was almost the first time I had ever been in a boat, though I was nineteen years old. From that time till his death he went on, loyal and brave, without spot or blemish or any such thing, loving and loved. He

HON. ELIHU B. WASHBURNE.
Secretary of State and Minister to France 1869–77.

had seen the vision and he walked with God. He came perfectly naturally into our calling of the ministry. Wherever he was he made a circle of youngsters who loved him and perhaps worshipped him, and so he lifted them into the Higher Life.

When I made that visit, his charming sisters were in the home. One of them, who left us not long ago, married into the Greenleaf family.

I think Henry Longfellow was there at the same time. I have tried to express in public once and again the blessing which he brought to Harvard College. I mark its history with a line for the day when he came there, only twenty-nine years old. Since that day teacher and pupil, professor and undergraduate, have been of one heart and one soul. Up till that time the etiquette required that a professor should not recognize the existence of a pupil in the College yard. Since that time it has been *we* who are going to do this, *we* who have done that, freshman and dean are all one in the "honorable company of letters." For here was this young fellow,

Henry Longfellow, who was not only to teach us but to quicken us and inspire us and make us glad that we were admitted into the secrets of learning and literature. He would walk with us when we took our constitutional, he would play a game of whist with us if we met together at Mrs. Eliot's. He changed the routine of his part of the College from the routine of the class room to the courtesies and cordialities of a parlor.

And it would take a volume to record what Longfellow was in the amenities and charities of home life. Till he died that old Washington house of his at Cambridge was, one might say, the trysting-place of every tramp from France, or Spain, or Bohemia, or Mesopotamia, or the parts of Libya around Cyrene, who could not speak the English language, and who wanted bread for his mouth and clothes for his back. And not one of these beggars was ever turned away. I believe I never knew but one nobleman of sixteen quarterings. After the days when exiles could return home, he died in his castle on the Danube where his grandfather's grandfather had been born.

This man was introduced to me by Henry Longfellow, whom he knew because he had gone to him

JAMES G. BLAINE.
From a photograph by Sarony.

starving and half naked, in need of everything, and with no claim upon Longfellow but that he had suffered with Kossuth in his country's cause.

They tell me that there are more English men and English women who read and know Longfellow's verses than there are who read and know Tennyson's in the same island. I do not know if this is so. But I can see that it might be so. It is a great thing to be the poet of the People. Do you remember how Dr. Holmes reminded us that Isaac Watts is quoted twenty times every day for once when a line of Pope or Dryden is repeated?

But we are to look in at the windows of other places, upon the faces of other people, and for the moment we must bid good-by to the state of Maine.

"And you have come so far," said one of the readers of this chapter when it was first printed, "and you have said nothing about the 'Maine Law'?" Yet it is that law which has given the name of Maine to the world of English-speaking people, and half the people who will ever speak to me about Maine will speak to me to ask about it. Very well, this is no place to discuss its theory or to go into the details of practice; it will be enough if I repeat, what is true, what this same James Gillespie Blaine said of the Maine Law, "It found Maine a poor state and it left her a rich one."

ARNOLD'S MARCH *through the* WILDERNESS
The Americans under Gen. Arnold, penetrated though an unexplored Wilderness to Quebec. in the Fall of 1775. after severe difficulties and privations

FROM AN OLD PRINT

CHAPTER III

NEW HAMPSHIRE

PERSONS or places? Why, both persons and places, if you please, gentle reader. If you please, for places we can go up to the Tip Top House on Mount Washington, which, before we knew of the North Carolina mountains, we called the highest land east of the Mississippi. Or for persons we can go to Graduation Day at Exeter and see the young American who means to sway the rod of empire in 1935.

And here am I, your guide and mentor. The first time I stood at the Tip Top House was at ten o'clock at night in the first week of September, 1841, with a crowbar in my hand as I pressed upon the door. It was after a tramp from Randolph which had lasted seventeen hours and had taken us over Jefferson and through one or two thunderstorms. The last time I arrived there I was with an old friend on the back seat of a victoria, with four horses before us who had trotted most of the way from the Alpine House. And the at-

MOUNT WASHINGTON, AND THE WHITE HILLS.
(From near Crawford's.)

From an engraving of about the time of Dr. Hale's first ascent.

tentive keeper of the Tip Top House ran forward.

"Is this you, Dr. Hale? I am so sorry you are just too late for our dinner, but you shall have something to eat by the time you are ready. Would you rather have hot chops, or would you rather have some tenderloin steak?

We will make you as comfortable as we can."

This is what happens when fifty years go by. And literally one of my last visits in New Hampshire was on that day, a pathetic day as it proved, which Exeter boys will long remember. We dedicated to good learning and high patriotism two noble buildings which George Shattuck Morison had cared for and for which I believe he paid, —George Morison, the king of American engineers. He died a few weeks after, leaving for us two or three leading studies of American duty which must not be forgotten.

Yes, it is just as it was in Maine. You can box the compass. Things? If you want things, you can have them on a large scale. Men? If you want men, why, we have Daniel Webster. We will not say in this connection here, we have Franklin Pierce. On a small scale, remember that somewhere I have said something of a baby three months of age who was attended by Mrs. Jeremiah Smith when she was Miss Hale, a charming girl of seventeen, who came to visit my dear mother in the public house of Dover.

My father, with some scientific friends, was at that moment attacking "the Notch," as we used to call it, as if there were no other, and ascending by the early pioneer path to the summit of Mount Washington. Year by year people found out how attractive all that region is.

To me, personally, after I saw it on the Geological Survey of New Hampshire in 1841, it became a duty as it became a privilege to go up every summer and thread those forests again. The glory of forests is more than the glory of mountains. I remember I used to say that if the time came of a summer when I did not want to go to New Hampshire, I knew I was out of order somehow and ought to go. And with the first two minutes of forest life Nature asserted herself and I was well again.

If any one wants to travel in New Hampshire and see the central wonders as they revealed themselves to Darby Field, that original Irishman who came up here in 1642, let him make roughly on the margin of this page the letter M.

Then, if he is a New Yorker, he may say: "I will go up by the vertical stroke of the left hand of the M, and I there come to Bethlehem. I will go down from Bethlehem through the Notch till I come to Intervale. I will go up

THE DIXVILLE NOTCH.
From a photograph copyright, 1900, by the Detroit Photographic Co.

again from Intervale by Pinkham's Notch to Gorham and the Alpine House, and then I will go down on the right-hand vertical of the M and I shall come to Sebago Pond and beautiful Bridgton, and go to Portland, the most charming of New England cities excepting Burlington."

Now, if he choose, he may go down from Bethlehem through the valley of the Pemigewasset. He may go up to Waterville, highest inhabited land in New England. He may go down to Squam Lake, and see my boys on Harry Sawyer's farm; he may cruise on Winnepesaukee as long as he chooses, and he may go across on foot or on his donkey through Tamworth, Conway, and again to Intervale. He will find Intervale a good centre with memories of old artist days.

But there are other regions to be traversed. You must not venture to talk about New Hampshire till you have been through the Dixville Notch. If you have the real Bohemian spirit in you, you will take a birch canoe (which, believe me, is better than a cedar) at Connecticut Lake, the head of Connecticut River.[1] Why not look in on Senator Spooner if the Senate has

[1] This is as good a place as any to say that Connecticut means a long tidal river, and that the experts spell it quinnehtukqut. Winthrop bought corn in the Connecticut Valley the first year after his people came here.

adjourned? You will come out sunburnt and strong at Saybrook on Long Island Sound. Or, after three or four weeks of happy adventure on Connecticut River, you will go across to Rangeley and try there for salmon trout or

ON THE PRESIDENTIAL RANGE.

for salmon. You will find one or two Senators there; or you will study the grandeur of their Lake Country there; or you will wander in the quarries of granite which are just on the eastern side of the line of Maine, but more accessible from New Hampshire.

At Diana's Bath, or Pigwacket, there is much which Pan and the Oreads and Naiads have to show you; and, as the Pope says of Rome, after you have been with us some years, you will find that you know nothing.

And now as for Men, on the other hand. These people always had a sturdy habit of their own. We people in Boston Bay sent them into exile when we made an end of Anne Hutchinson and the other Mystics and Progressives of her time. For the first and the last time in New England, what men now call a Presbytery sat on the First Church in Boston in 1636, and the Commonwealth was foolish enough to send into exile the most intelligent members of that Church in Boston, and left only a few dozen at home to pick up the pieces and make Boston out of them as well as they could. So these people, whose names are Maude, Wheelwright, and Pormort, among others, with a half-dozen more, went beyond the Massachusetts line to Exeter and Dover and Portsmouth. I may say, in passing, that they pronounced Portsmouth as if it were

Porchmouth, and their true descendants speak so to this day. It was Strawberry Bank then.

Well, sometimes these exiles wanted the strong arm of Massachusetts to help them, and then they always had it. An ancestor of mine, Captain John Everett, commanded the train-bands of Massachusetts Bay there for a generation when Jesuits and Algonquins were too much for the settlers. But, on the other hand, whenever they chose, they had an assembly of their own and did very much as they pleased, and I think that is their habit to this day.

ELEAZAR WHEELOCK.
From a painting in the possession of Dartmouth College.

Among other pieces of independence was the revolution in the great Democratic party, by which in 1843 and 1844 New Hampshire became the first in point of time of American states to make an anti-slavery platform, while up to that time, in a spirit of local independence, she had always chosen to give a Democratic vote and so to ally herself to the Southern hierarchy. When it came to the annexation of Texas, however, the Democrats of New Hampshire said "No!" and instead of voting steadily in the Southern column, they went over and laid the advance for freedom.

One of the pioneers, whose name, Eleazar Wheelock, is hardly remembered, took it into his head before the American Revolution to found a college which was to be especially for the "education of Indians for the service of Christ." Mr. Edwin D. Mead reminds me that Wheelock was educated at New Haven as one of the scholars who were there supported by Berkeley's bounty. It was thus, as it proved, that Berkeley established his American college.

"Westward the star of empire takes its way."

Wheelock went to England, and there he found favor with Lord Dartmouth, the one member of Lord North's Cabinet who was "pure, peaceable, gentle, and easy to be entreated, given to mercy and good works, without partiality and without hypocrisy." And the Earl of Dartmouth was good to the Indian apostle, who named his college Dartmouth College in his memory. In a diary of that century I find it called Dresden College. They tell me that while I write,[1] the present Earl of Dartmouth is girding on his armor and preparing to take an ocean voyage to see the Dartmouth College of to-day. "A little college," Daniel Webster said. "But she has children who love her."

Portsmouth? Yes. All of you have read Miss Jewett's novel, "The Tory Lover," or if you have not, you will thank me for telling you to do so. There you get a bit of Paul Jones, and in Mr. Buell's history, which reveals so much to

[1] Since the words were written above, the Earl of Dartmouth has made his auspicious visit to Dartmouth College. The new generation was delighted to honor him, and he and his party have left the most agreeable remembrances behind them.

Lord Dartmouth.
From a painting in the possession of Dartmouth College.

us, you have Paul Jones at greater length and so at much greater advantage. What a pity it is that we have lost Mr. Buell just as we discovered that we had another historian! In their enthusiasm for Paul Jones the Continental Congress ordered that the plan should be drawn and the timber collected with which to build a ship of the line, *America*, which was to be the flagship of this great American seaman. No more rotten *Poor Richards* for him. He shall have an American ship built from American woods for an American seaman. Thirty-two years before, Portsmouth had built a frigate *America* for the English navy, but we shall have an *America* of our own. The new ship of the line was just about finished, I have a right to say probably the finest vessel of her class in the world, when the French king's ship, the *Magnifique*, ran against a rock in Boston Harbor and sank. I am afraid her bones are there to this day. And the fickle Congress forgot its own Admiral, gave the *America* to "our illustrious ally," and McCarthy, commander of the *Magnifique*, took his sailors down to Portsmouth to superintend her fitting for the ocean. Here I have his Log Book of those days, if you would only read it, but, alas! you do not care for history.

Her after history is given to me very kindly by Mr. Gauss, of our Navy Department. It appears that in 1793 she sailed under Admiral Sercy from Brest for Santo Domingo, to convoy loaded merchant vessels ready to return to France. This and other ships of the French navy were detained in the West Indies, owing to the insurrection in Santo Domingo and other causes, until June 24, 1793, when Admiral Sercy started out with his fleet. Some of them are mentioned by name as coming to the United States ports for supplies, and some are named as reaching Brest late in November, 1793. The next summer, on the celebrated first of June, when Lord Howe beat the French squadron off Ushant, she was taken into the British navy and named the *Impétueux*. This change was made because they had already an *America*. The French ship *Impétueux*, which had been taken at Ushant, had been burned at Portsmouth, England, and her name *Impétueux* was given to this larger *America* in commemoration of the French ship.

As *L'Impétueux* she became a favorite ship in the English navy. They told me at the Admiralty that when Lord Exmouth (Sir Edward Pellew) was to command the fleet, he chose *L'Impétueux* as his flagship.

JOHN PAUL JONES.
From the original miniature in the United States Naval Institute, Annapolis, Md.

All this I have said in such detail because the late Mr. Buell, in his invaluable life of Paul Jones, had been misled. He says that King Louis changed the name of our *America* into the *Franklin*. Now, the *Franklin* was the ship captured at Aboukir by Lord Nelson. She was considered the finest two-deck ship in the world, but she is not our *America*. And it is a pity that this mistake should have worked its way into literature. Our American *Impétueux* is sometimes rated as a seventy-four-gun ship and sometimes as seventy-eight.

But poor Paul Jones was left lamenting because we wanted to make a present to "our illustrious ally."

In my own earlier days, camping for a night under a white pine and an open sky, I remember an old forester told me that he had seen the broad arrow of King George on pines in that forest which were too far from water to be carried to the Merrimac. I think it quite likely that some old Appalachian may find King George's broad arrow at this day.

The Appalachian Club of New England is an excellent club. Semiramis says that it is the only club in Boston which has a real *raison d'être*. Perhaps this is true. Anyway, it brings together young men and maidens, wise men and people who know as little as I do, but who love the open air, who are not afraid to be alone with

God, and so are willing, if need be, to lie on hemlock boughs with a fire burning a cord of wood at one's feet, and look up on the sky. Now this Appalachian Club does not satisfy itself with stereoscopic pictures in winter or sonnets addressed to robin redbreasts or the starry canopy. But it sends into the wilderness such men as Mr. Edmands, and as my friends the Lowes, to make paths to and establish camps and leave water-mugs for the benefit of wayfarers, and sometimes an enthusiast gives them a few cents or a few dollars with which to buy a few pine trees to preserve them for posterity. Blessings on the Appalachian Club, and blessings on the Forestry Association of New Hampshire! Let the reader reflect that the Soracte mines gave him ten per cent last month instead of seven, and let him send that extra three per cent which he does not know what to do with to the treasurer of the Appalachian and bid him buy a little bit of pine forest for the benefit of the reader's great-grandson

THE BROAD ARROW.

in 1975, and let that great-grandson take this volume out from the library and thank me for the suggestion.

Do not fear to come up here from New Padua, from Baltimore, from Knoxville, from New Orleans, or from Waco. We have a fine set of guides, who know what they are about, who neither drink, nor swear, nor steal, nor play "high-low," but who love to make you love the forests and the mountains. Let it be for only twenty-four hours if you please, or let it be for six months if you please. Put yourself fairly into the forest reserve, to see what there is to be seen, to eat what there is to eat, to do what there is to do, and to enjoy all there is to enjoy, and then you will not need to read our papers on New Hampshire.

And, not to let this chapter pass without saying something of persons as well as places, let me counsel my pupil to spend time enough at Dartmouth College to understand what is the charm that it has for everybody. It is under the direction of one of the first educators of our

Dartmouth College.
From an old engraving.

time, Dr. Tucker. From the time of John Ledyard (who is now forgotten, as he ought not to be) to these days, when so many of our active statesmen hark back to their happy years at Dartmouth, it has been gaining on the right hand and on the left hand, above and below, behind and before. Never were more august ceremonies than those of the hundredth anniversary of Daniel Webster's Commencement. Never have people loved their Alma Mater more than Webster did, than Choate did, or Ticknor, or Field, or some of these younger men who are on the stage to-day. With great good sense, the government of the College manages to connect its scientific school with the necessities

Dr. William Jewett Tucker.
President of Dartmouth College.

of the times. With great good sense, they have administered their College so that study and learning, science and literature, are still the fashion as the foundation there.

This is a good place to repeat the story which the late Senator Patterson told me upon the spot. He took me to the magnificent elm which stands at one corner of the open common in Hanover and made me remark the exquisite beauty of twenty or more branches as they rise and curve and bend toward the ground. It is one of the noble specimens of the American elm which justifies well Michaux's remark that the American elm is queen of the forests of the world. Mr. Patterson told me that when he himself was a student he assisted one of the professors who bound together a number of little elms, each as big as your thumb perhaps, and planted them together in this corner of the quadrangle. They have grown together and are now one tree.

As for the Academy at Exeter, it won its honors early, and it holds them with pride to this day. One of the Phillipses of Andover endowed the school, and he builded a great deal better than he knew. No boys are better fitted for college than its pupils are. And the reason is that somehow the true democratic principle has intrenched itself there, and a fellow is really

PHILLIPS EXETER ACADEMY.

esteemed as he attends to the business for which academies and colleges are founded. One of the school's accomplished instructors said to me once that nothing was more pathetic than to watch the first three months of a boy who comes to Exeter supposing that he is going to fool away his father's money and his own time in a series of sports, where the studies are only exceptions. You might make a Greek tragedy, almost, out of the struggle of such a boy with his old self when he finds that work, and hard work, is the business of the place.

The Revolutionary history of New Hampshire would make an excellent book if one of the new school of historians would take it up and would illustrate it. I like to spend a month every summer in Conway. Well, why is Conway called Conway? Because General Henry Seymour Conway stood up for the colonists so well in the discussions of the English Parliament and the Stamp Act. The town of Boston asked Conway for his portrait for Faneuil Hall, and he sent it to them; and General Howe stole it when he went away, and no man knows where the real portrait is to-day. But a better monument for Conway is in the lovely summer home of the people who breathe God's air there.

John Stark, the New Hampshire general, at the rail fence at Bunker Hill, must have seen, eye to eye, William Howe, the English general who attacked him and was repelled there. The Stark regiment covered the retreat on that day which men thought so fatal to the American army. When Howe addressed his men before

FIELD-MARSHAL CONWAY.
From an engraving of 1798.

attacking the American works, he said he would ask them to go no farther than he went himself; and in fact he marched on foot with the regiment by the side of its colonel. They attacked Stark and the New Hampshire regiment who were, as we New Englanders say, "behind the rail fence." The New Hampshire firing was so severe that the English regiment gave way, and it proved when the day was over that every officer of the Forty-second was killed or wounded. Howe alone bore a charmed life. And one of the letters of the time says that his white silk stockings were bloody from the blood on the grass as he retreated with the rest.

Stark afterward thought that the Continental Congress had slighted him, so when he cut off Baum and his party at Bennington, he made the report of his victory to the state of New Hampshire and to the General Court of Massachusetts but not to the Congress at Philadelphia. We preserve in the Massachusetts State House the "one Hessian gun and bayonet, one broadsword, one brass-barrelled drum," which Stark sent us after that day. It is rather interesting to know how people did such things then; so I will put on record the resolution in which the "Board of War" was instructed "to present to the Honourable Brigadier-general Stark a complete suit of clothes becoming his rank, together with a piece of linen as

JOHN STARK.

testimony of the high sense this Court have of the great and important services rendered by that officer."

Did any one think to send Admiral Dewey a

new uniform on the 1st of May, 1898? My own little tribute to Stark is in the marching song of Stark's men as he took them down to Bennington, or, as he called it, Wollomsac. If we can trust Colonel Creasy, the history of Bennington and what followed belongs in the history of the fifteen great battles of the world.

THE MARCHING SONG OF STARK'S MEN[1]

March! March! March! from sunrise till it's dark,
And let no man straggle on the way!
March! March! March! as we follow old John Stark,
For the old man needs us all to-day.

Load! Load! Load! Three buckshot and a ball,
With a hymn-tune for a wad to make them stay!
But let no man dare to fire till he gives the word to all
Let no man let the buckshot go astray.

Fire! Fire! Fire! Fire all along the line,
When we meet them bloody Hessians in array!
They shall have every grain from this powder-horn of mine,
Unless the cowards turn and run away!

[1] My accomplished friend, Mr. Whelpley, has set this marching song to music for the benefit of the New Hampshire schoolboys. If you are reading the Bible, you do not say "marching song," but a "song of degrees."

Home! Home! Home! When the fight is fought and
won,
To the home where the women watch and pray!
To tell them how John Stark finished what he had begun,
And to hear them thank our God for the day.

August 16, 1777.

These latter years are years of mourning for us who love New Hampshire, because this new business of paper pulp is stripping off her magnificent forests.

In old times, as I have said, King George sent his surveyors round, and when they saw a tree fit for his navy, they marked it with the broad arrow of the navy, so when its time came it was cut down in the winter, was hauled on the snow to the largest stream within range, and floated down to the ocean. I think it could be shown that in all the great sea fights in which the English, French, Spanish, or American navies were engaged between 1776 and 1790, the spars of all the vessels were from the New Hampshire forests. So other ship-builders cut logs and floated them down if they were big enough for spars or wide enough for boards. But the smaller trees were left,

> "Not for the good they may do now,
> But will do when they're grown up."

So that the mountains were still green, and so the forests still grew into cathedral aisles. And with every summer the wilderness was alive with glories for which there is no comparison.

Then, alas! Satan came walking up and down. And he devised methods of making paper from wood pulp. Before him, when angels and archangels presided over that business, paper was made of such rags as busy housewives minded to see the end of, and haply of older paper which had served its turn.

But now, alas! there is not a tree in the forest, big or little, old or young, from which you cannot make paper.

What follows is that you enter your forest with your axes in summer as you once did in winter, and you cut down virtually everything. If you leave a few sumach bushes or blackberry vines, it is because they are not worth the handling, they are so small. Big pines, little pines, big spruces, little spruces, big hemlock, little hemlock, — all fall before the axe. All is grist for Satan's mill.

For which the remedy will come — so soon as the Congress of America makes a National Park of the White Mountain summits. The state has surveyed the region carefully, and a fit plan has been prepared. Uncle Sam must acquire fifty square miles, be the same more or less, and put it in charge of his foresters. And then my children's children's children shall see the great-grandchildren of the pines that I saw sixty years ago, in place of the sumach and other rubbish that the pulp creatures have left us to-day. We ought to have done this years ago, but it is not too late for the twenty-first century.

CHAPTER IV

VERMONT

VERMONT is a region of wonderful picturesque beauty. The fields are very fertile, and it has proved to have great agricultural resources. For myself, I have never seen fields of clover which compared with the rich clover fields of Vermont when clover is in blossom. I suppose there are such fields elsewhere, but I never saw them. All the same, the first English settlement of Vermont was as late as the year 1724, when Fort Dummer, in the southern part of the state, was established by the province of Massachusetts. But, as has been said, no considerable number of settlers went in until the Peace of 1762 made that frontier of New England secure against foreign invasion. It was a frontier state, and, as I said in speaking of Maine just now, it was a field of war, not of peace.

THE GREEN MOUNTAINS.

For some reason or other there were no native residents there at the time when our first white colonists landed, so men say. It seems to have been, I think, by a sort of common consent on the part of the Indians who lived in New Hampshire, Massachusetts, and New York, that when, in hunting, the Indians met each other there they did not cut each other's throats. I am apt to think, however, also, that if a party of Iroquois crossed from central New York into that region, they would have fought against the Indians of New England, who were their standing enemies. Remember that the Iroquois vocabulary was absolutely different from that of the New England tribes, and all their methods of social life and their warfare differed. Has any one ever heard of a New England Indian burning a prisoner to death, as the Iroquois undoubtedly often did?

Anyway, what is sure is that there was no resident population of Indians in what we call Vermont, though in summer they went down to Lake Champlain, having fished and hunted deer up and down through the valleys.

While the New Hampshire mountains rest mostly on granite, the mountain range of the Green Mountains which runs through Vermont rests on slates and shales which are often tipped up almost perpendicularly.

So it happens that the mountains of Vermont are more picturesque, on the whole, than are the New Hampshire mountains. That sort of puddingy aspect which people criticise in our dear Mount Washington hardly appears in the Green Mountains. For the same reason the river gorges are more like the cañons of the West than any other valleys in New England. The story is a familiar one of the country doctor who, pressing his horse home at midnight over a bridge which he had crossed by daylight, found the horse very unwilling to go. It proved next day that he had pressed the horse along a stringpiece of the

General Wolfe.

"VIEW OF THE TAKING OF QUEBECK BY THE ENGLISH FORCES COMMANDED BY GENERAL WOLFE, SEPTEMBER 13TH, 1759."

From an old copperplate engraving published in London in 1760.

bridge, from which the boards had been washed away since he passed early in the day. This story is told, perfectly authenticated, I should say, of one of the streams which flows into Lake Champlain. It is told just as well authenticated in Berkshire County in Massachusetts. And a correspondent tells me that the same story is told of the Ausable River in New York. The reader may judge whether the same thing happened three times. What I know is that it might have happened at any of these gorges. The walls of the torrent in all cases are a sort of slaty shale which rises perpendicular from the water.

The civilized history of Vermont begins only when the incursions of Indians and Jesuits ceased with Wolfe's victory at Quebec. Then began an enthusiasm for settlement of those beautiful valleys. There are still extant the records of the parties which were sent from one or another town of Connecticut, Massachusetts, or New Hampshire, and some of their marching songs. Thus there grew up the sturdy set of Green Mountain boys who give such picturesqueness to the history of that whole region. In 1777 the English governors of Canada hoped that they should seduce these people from allegiance to the Continental Congress, which had never done anything for them. An officer of rank was imprudent enough to try to seduce Ethan Allen when Allen was a prisoner in New York. He told Allen that he should be the colonel of a regiment, should be presented to the king, and should have "a large tract of land either in the New Hampshire Grants or in Connecticut." Ethan Allen replied: "I told him that if by faithfulness I had recom-

ETHAN ALLEN.
"In the Name of the Great Jehovah and the Continental Congress!"

mended myself to General Howe, I should be loath by unfaithfulness to lose the governor's good opinion. Besides that, I viewed the offer of land to be similar to that which the devil offered Jesus Christ, 'to give him all the kingdoms of the world if he would fall down and worship him,' when at the same time the damned soul had not a foot of land on earth."

From that day to this day Vermont has earned the name, among people who know anything about it, of a model democracy. I wish that one of the intelligent Swiss writers on government would come over here to see how they do things in Vermont. You see, there are no very large cities. Burlington, the largest of them all, is a model city for the world to take note of and keep in memory.

I like to put in here a description of Burlington which I made in a speech before Alpha Delta Phi at its annual convention in New York in 1888. I had had, not long before, a friendly passage with Matthew Arnold, who had said rather carelessly that there was nothing "distinguished" in America.

"When I heard in conversation this criticism, which I had never seen in print, about the absence of anything 'distinguished' in our cities, I asked myself what was the last American city I had visited in my winter travels. As it happened, it was one of the smallest of American cities —

VIEW OF BURLINGTON, VERMONT.
From an old copperplate engraving.

the city of Burlington, in the state of Vermont. I may be told that there was nothing distinguished there. Perhaps not; but I know that, as we entered the town, as I looked back on the Green Mountains, which had been white with snow all day, but were now rosy red in the glory of the setting sun, I thought it was one of the noblest visions I had ever looked upon. I turned to look upon the clouds of sunset — to see, far away, the sun as he went down between the broken range of the Adirondack Mountains. Between was the white ice of Lake Champlain. So far as Nature has anything to offer to the eye, I had certainly never seen in the travels of forty years any position chosen for a city more likely to impress a traveller as remarkable, and to live always in his memory. I had been summoned to Burlington on an errand connected with the public administration of charity. It was supposed that, as I came from Boston, I knew how cities ought to be governed. Anyway, I was up there as an expert. Now, what was the chief thing I found? Those of you who have ever been in Burlington will know that I was in a city of palaces. I mean by that, that there are private homes there, which, while they have the comforts of a log cabin, display the elegances of a palace. But I shall be told that this is not distinguished now — that this may be seen everywhere in a country as rich as America. Let it be so. Then they took me to visit a new hospital, arranged with everything which modern science knows for the treatment of disease, with a staff of surgeons and physicians who might stand unawed before the great leaders in their profession; and they told me that here any person in Vermont who was in need could be treated by the best science of the nineteenth century, and with the tenderest care which the Christian religion inspires. They told me that this institution was maintained by a fund of nearly half a million dollars, given by one lady, for this purpose of blessing her brothers and sisters of mankind. If this be a commonplace monument, let us thank God that we live in a commonplace land. They took me then to the public library. They showed me the Canadian immigrants from the other side of the border thronging the passages that each might have his French book to read, the German immigrant pressing for his book; they showed a perfect administration for the supply of these needs.

And they showed me that they had not only provided for the rank and file in this way — providing, observe, thousands of books in German and thousands of books in French — but they showed the 'last sweet thing' in the criticism of Dante, the last publications of the archæological societies of Italy, — books and prints which had been issued, well, let us say it among ourselves, for as dainty people as you and I are, for the elegant students of Browning or of mediæval times. They had taken as good care of us in our daintiness as they had taken of the Canadian wood-chopper or of the German mechanic. This seemed to me rather a distinguished bit of administration. And so I might go on to tell you about other arrangements for charities, of their forelook in regard to sanitary arrangements. And when I asked them on the particular matter where I was sent for to give counsel — how many people they had in their Blackwell's Island establishments, in their public institutions for the poor — I found there was a momentary question whether there were three of these people at that moment in these public institutions, or possibly four!

"That is so distinguished a condition of affairs that I should not dare tell the story in any social science congress in Europe. It would be set down as a Yankee exaggeration. People would say it was impossible. It is not impossible, because the men and women of Burlington have known how to give themselves to the administration of 'the wealth in common.' Among other things, I may say, in passing, that they have known how to suppress the open bar."

To the reader at a distance, who knows nothing of New England life, it will be as well to say that such homage as I am thus paying to Vermont is a homage to Local Government. What in Vermont we call republican democracy, or democratic republicanism, results in such a picture as I have here printed of Burlington. It is what Kropotkin and his friends would call "anarchy," by which they mean strongly accented local government with no central power. Given a region of intelligent men, and men who love God and wish to serve him, a region where most people live where they have lived since childhood, a region where everybody can read and write; and let the people of such a region take care of themselves, of their own schools, their own roads, their own poorhouses, without the interference of any central authority, and you come out on the state of Vermont, or something like it.

I happened to be the witness of a very pretty little incident in which some of "them furreners" learned what it is so hard for them to learn, that while you live in a democracy you may be subject to Law, and that this Law has a very large L. It seems that for some sorts of charcoal you need some sorts of wood. For instance, if you are going to make an annealed watch spring, you do not use the same charcoal as if you were making steel rails at ninety-nine pounds a yard. So one of the great charcoal burners of the world had bought a few thousand acres, more or less, of woodland in Vermont to meet the wishes of some particular customers. To cut down the wood and burn it a commander of Dagoes had brought up a little regiment of Dagoes, and they went to work. After they had been at work a year or more, there appeared the tax collector of the town with his bills for the poll-tax of every Dago among them. Now the paying of taxes was just one of the things which the Dago had meant to avoid by leaving the beneficent reign of King Victor Emmanuel, or whoever it was. So they said when the tax bills came in that they would be hanged if they would pay them. I am not sure but that they used expressions more theological. To them the tax collector merely replied, very much to their surprise, that if they did not pay them, the whole

SAMUEL DE CHAMPLAIN.

army of Vermont would appear if necessary on the scene, and they would all be sent to prison.

I tell this story because it was a perfect eye-opener to these Dagoes. The man who moved them to and fro, as you move chessmen on a board, said that he would do whatever the Consul General of Italy in the city of New York said he must do. Observe, and this is the interesting point with me, the way in which the Celt steadily holds to his disposition to be governed by a Boss. Somebody went down to New York; the Consul General was no fool, and he told them they must pay their poll-taxes and they paid them. They got their first lesson as to the strength of a Democratic Republic.

In old days the annual session of the legislature ranged from three days to ten. But I am told now the legislature meets only on alternate years. It meets in the early part of September and usually sits till the last of November. I had the pleasure of meeting one of Vermont's governors once for a few days at a hotel in western North Carolina. Every morning at breakfast he brought in the business of the state of Vermont in an envelope in which he had received it from the secretary of state, and the lieutenant-governor. The whole of it could be transmitted for four cents' worth of postage. This governor, if the Philistines want to know, had a salary of a thousand dollars a year, and if it were necessary for his wife's health or for his own studies that he should spend a month in western North Carolina, why, he could do so, leaving details to the lieutenant-governor. What this gentleman needed to consult the governor about could be transacted, as I saw, through the Post Office. Happy is that people whose history is not written! Happy is that people whose legislative sessions are few and short! Happy is that state which always votes the Republican ticket! They invented a new motto for their state some fifty years ago, "The star which never sets." This means that from the beginning they never gave in to the Southern Oligarchy in any matter of form or of principle.

There are many, many ways to see Vermont.

Defeat of the Iroquois at Lake Champlain.

A facsimile of Champlain's engraving, in the 1613 edition of his "Voyages."

There are many, many pleasant places to visit in Vermont. Go, if you please, to Atherton, an imaginary town which I invented for my unread novel, "Sybil Knox." For myself, I never enjoyed life more than I did when, in 1864, I started with my haversack from the mouth of the Ashuelot River and walked across to Burlington and Lake Champlain. I could make a book about my memories of that walk, of the persons who joined me, of the scenery, and of the glorious prosperity of the free people.

The earliest history of Vermont carries us back to the very beginning of the seventeenth century.

When Champlain was doing his best to get through to the Pacific Ocean, he discovered the lake which bears his name. Somewhere at the southern end of that lake he and the Indians who escorted him had a skirmish with some other Indians who were perhaps Iroquois. It is not possible to place the incident of these early adventures of his.

The state as we found of New Hampshire has a

Revolutionary history which is well worth following; of those who are remembered, and as the Book of Ecclesiasticus says, of those others who were not remembered.

BRIGADIER-GENERAL SIMON FRASER, LIEUTENANT-COLONEL OF THE 24TH FOOT.
1729–1777.

(General Fraser commanded the British forces at the battle of Hubbardton.)

Let me tell the story of one Vermont battle-field, because it brings in the pathetic story of one of my own kinsmen, and these chapters are chapters not only of places but of persons. This is the story of the Nathan Hale who was taken prisoner by Burgoyne's land forces at Hubbardton.

The Massachusetts contingent had been hurried up to meet Burgoyne. John Stark, who was a sort of Agamemnon sulking in his tent, was bringing up the New Hampshire militia, and he eventually commanded at Bennington. But the force which practically met Burgoyne was a force of militia who were entirely outnumbered. They knew as much of military tactics as the reader of these words knows, perhaps a little more. But they knew how to fight, and they knew how to die.

The Earl of Balcarras and Burgoyne, in their testimony before the House of Lords, spoke with admiration of the gallant behavior of these men at Hubbardton. They were entirely outnumbered in that fight, but they did not retire till an action so severe that the English lost one hundred and fifty men. There is not a bit of Revolutionary reading more interesting than Burgoyne's statement as to the spirit with which these men engaged. In his testimony before the House of Lords he makes occasion to say that any critic who thought that his antagonists were a horde of inexperienced peasants were greatly mistaken. He begs that it may be understood that he acted against soldiers who showed great spirit and courage.

In 1777 the king's government in England was fully satisfied that Burgoyne's expedition was to cut the rebel forces in two by his march from Montreal to New York; to leave New England out in the cold, and so to end the rebellion.

RUINS OF FORT TICONDEROGA.

Burgoyne had everything given to him which he wanted. Carleton, afterwards Lord Dorchester, had very nearly cleared Canada of the Rebel invasion in 1776, and Burgoyne advanced southward in a short triumph over Lake Champlain.

Hessians and English arrived at Ticonderoga at the southern end of the lake with no formidable naval opposition. It is then that the colors of England and Brunswick and Hesse

> "In triumph vain
> Gay flaunted over blue Champlain."

Millions had been spent on Fort Ticonderoga in one or another generation. To this hour the "ruins" are more like the ruins we read about than anything else which can be seen in the northern states of America. It was considered a great point of success when in 1775 Ethan Allen had surprised Ticonderoga and taken it for the colonies in the name of "Jehovah and the Continental Congress." When Burgoyne advanced, this fort was held by St. Clair for the Americans. It was a great disappointment to everybody when Burgoyne, by what seems to have been a surprise to St. Clair, planted his guns on Mount Defiance, which had been supposed inaccessible, and without firing a shot compelled St. Clair's garrison to retire. He could not ask for a more auspicious beginning of his invasion.

There is something very fine, I say, — it is what we call soldier-like, — in his narrative in the credit he gives to the spirit and discipline of the retreating force as it retired southward from Ticonderoga. A hundred and thirty years later it is worth while to contrast it with the unfair impression given at the time in New England. Because the Americans retreated, it was, perhaps, the habit of our people to say they ran away.

In fact, at the battle of Hubbardton, with two thousand men they engaged, according to Burgoyne's account, the advanced guard of the whole English army. Burgoyne says that they left dead on the field Colonel Francis and many other officers, with upwards of two hundred men, — that they lost six hundred in wounded. They lost also one colonel, seven captains, and two hundred and twenty other prisoners. It seems to me really pathetic that as well-fought a battle as this should appear in the popular notion of that time as a disgraceful retreat.

Nathan Hale, the colonel of one of the regi-

General Stark at the Battle of Bennington.

From an old engraving by J. R. Chapin of the painting by J. Godfrey.

ments, was taken prisoner. Burgoyne paroled him for two years which expired in 1779, when he loyally went to New York and surrendered himself on his parole. He died at New Utrecht, Long Island, just thirty-seven years old, three years after his cousin Nathan Hale, a Connecticut cousin, who was hanged in disgrace by General Howe, whose people had arrested him a few days before. This *Captain* Nathan Hale was hanged at the corner of the little park near Broadway. The disgrace of his being hanged rested on the whole Connecticut household from which he came. The method of his death was what they grieved for. My own father, who bore his uncle's name, was forbidden to speak of him to his father, because the whole was so painful. His one request when he was told that he must die was that he might be shot and not hanged. But now one of these Nathan Hales is remembered. There is a statue to him on Broadway. I stop to read the inscription every time I pass there: "I am sorry that I have but one life to give to my country;"

and I have never stopped there but some newsboy was at my side reading the same inscription. And the other of those Nathan Hales was never, I think, heard of by the reader of these lines till he reads them now. So far as fame goes, one of the two was taken and the other left, and the one who was taken was the one who thought he might be disgraced by the manner of his death.

The dates are these:—

General St. Clair abandoned Ticonderoga, 6th of July, 1777.

Battle of Hubbardton, 7th of July, 1777.

Battle of Bennington, August 16, 1777.

Battle of Saratoga, 19th of September, 1777.

Surrender at Saratoga, 17th of October, 1777.

In writing about New Hampshire I spoke of the battle of Bennington as belonging with Burgoyne's defeat at Saratoga. Colonel Creasy spoke of that as one of the fifteen decisive battles of the world. Bennington was in what was called the Hampshire Grants, which so soon declared their own independence and made Vermont a state which joined the old Thirteen when she chose.

Senator Hoar used to tell a fine story of his first visit to Bennington. He made some mistake in leaving his hotel to go to see the monument on the battle-ground. But he fell in with a

ALEXANDER MACOMB, MAJOR-GENERAL U. S. A.
From an engraving by J. B. Longacre of the painting by T. Sully.

little boy who became his guide. Hoar asked him some questions about the battle, and the boy was somewhat confused in his answers. He acknowledged that he was not perfectly informed, saying, "What I know is that the Benningtons beat." The actual battle-ground was on the New York side of the state line.

There is another feather in the cap of Vermont, which her own people prize perhaps, but outside her own borders it is not referred to so often as is that battle where the "Benningtons beat." This feather was won the day of the double battle of Plattsburg, in 1814, when General Macomb with his little army drove back Sir George Prevost with the English army, and when McDonough, only thirty years old, with the American fleet, sank or drove back the English fleet. That was one of the battles of ship-builders, as somebody calls them — Henry Adams, I think — when the question was, which nation could get a ship to sea before the other. McDonough's fleet went out almost as Æneas's went out from Carthage, with the green leaves growing on the end of their spars. Macomb's army was made up of such soldiers as he found. He had fifteen hundred "effectives," by which he means soldiers enlisted by the United States. McDonough did sink the great part of the English fleet, and drove the rest northward. On shore the English troops, before they made their main attack, heard the cheering of their American enemy on account of

Captain Thomas McDonough.
From an engraving by J. B. Forrest after a painting by J. W. Jarvis.

the defeat of the fleet, and so retreated — a retreat which went as far as Canada. Of course the repulse was appreciated at the time, when, indeed, it was greatly needed in America, for the capture of the city of Washington by Ross's army had taken place about a fortnight before. The effect of this repulse in England was practically that it ended the war.

The Ministry asked the Duke of Wellington to come over to America and to take the command. His answer is a very interesting letter, showing that he understood the condition more completely than some of those people who called themselves "the Government."

"Had any considerations of personal glory . . . induced me to pursue those offensive operations by land, independently of the fleet, which it would appear were expected of me," the results would have been disastrous, he says. Such operations have been attempted before on the same ground. And twenty-five years later he said that he "thought he sent them some of his best troops from Bordeaux, but they did not turn out quite right. They wanted this iron fist to command them." Condensing his various despatches declining to come over here and assume the command, it appears that we should consider that the critical battle of the whole concern was that in which McDonough and Macomb took command at Plattsburg. Observe the *Mac* in the name of the two commanders; and young men may as well observe that the sailor was thirty years old and the general was thirty-two years old. This reminds us of the young men of the Revolution.

Students and people who care for history, and people who care for the English language, and people who are glad that the United States *is* a nation, will not forget that George Perkins Marsh was a Vermonter, a man who rendered very great service to us all. He was very kind to me when I was a mere boy, and honored me by his correspondence till he died. And there is no better illustration than the statement of his career of the healthy and hearty results when you trust a nation to the insight and foresight of Democracy. In the old days of Southern supremacy, Vermont voted alone every year for the rule of free men in the nation, without what the politicians would call "reward."

She was the "star that never sets." But when General Taylor came in, and for a few years the

GEORGE PERKINS MARSH.
From the portrait by Healey painted in 1845.

men of business at the North ruled the land in place of the politicians of the South, it was thought at Washington that Vermont should be "rewarded," and they asked her representative, George Perkins Marsh, if he would accept a foreign mission.

Now, it happened that Marsh had been all his life studying the languages, the scenes, and the legends of northern Europe, and his friends intimated that it would be agreeable to him to represent this country at Copenhagen. Recollect that all this about Vinland and Thorfinn and Thorvald and the rest had just come to light. But the new government could not send him to Copenhagen, but said that they would send him to Constantinople. Scandinavian or Semitic — what difference did that make as the dice-box of patronage threw out its six or its five! And indeed that happened, if anything happens, that this master of Northern literature took in as a matter of course the Oriental questions and added the treasures of the East to the stock which seemed ample before. His philological learning gave him preëminence in the great diplomatic circle of Constantinople.

He afterwards travelled in the north of

Europe; he spent many years in Italy, to the great advantage of us all, and in philological matters which relate to our own language he is one

Mrs. George Perkins Marsh.

of the great leaders. But I do not like to speak of him without speaking of his charming wife, who made additions not to be forgotten to the literature of the century.

I think that the young men and young women of Vermont who want a college training are apt to go to their own colleges, Burlington and Middlebury, and that they are wise in doing so. I dare not go into the successes of Vermont's sons and daughters in literature. Everybody remembers, not to speak of persons now living in this country whose names and work we read every day, Saxe, and the Stevenses, Henry and Benjamin Franklin, to whom we owe inestimable contributions to American history. Vermont adopted Mr. Kipling, though he has run away from us for the moment.

Take care, while you are in Vermont, to see the great Proctor marble quarries. There is a town of Proctor, where some of them are. But I do not know how far their marvellous enterprise extends. I do know that Richard Greenough told me that the statuary marble of Vermont was equal to any in the world. And I think one or two of his best works preserve the memory of — what shall I say? — the blush or the sunset hue which just redeems the pure white from chill.

Senator Proctor's service to the country when the Cuban war began will never be forgotten.

And if you visit him this summer, let him know that you remember that Vermont gave the Morgan horse to the country. For the senator has highly determined that that race of horses shall not die out from the land.

Com.r Macdonoughs Farm-House, on Cumberland bay, Lake Champlain:
in the Dist.e are the American Forts, Town of Plattsburgh, River Saranac, the British Camp & head q.rs of S.r Geo. Provost.

THE STATE HOUSE.

"What Dr. Holmes audaciously called the 'hub of the Universe.'"

CHAPTER V

MASSACHUSETTS

A YEAR or two before Champlain was discovering Bar Harbor and Lake Champlain, the Earl of Southampton, whom the reader and I ought to love, sent a Captain named Gosnold to discover our dear New England. For the young noblemen of Queen Elizabeth's time were an enterprising and adventurous set. They meant to beat the devil by checkmating Spain, and they thought a good way to checkmate Spain and the devil would be to plant Protestant colonies in North America. So the Earl of Southampton sent out Gosnold in a ship of happy omen, for she was called the *Concord*.

PINE-TREE SHILLING.

And Gosnold came up and saw our dear old Boston. And he sailed round Cape Cod, which people once called Cape Gosnold, in memory of him. And he discovered the Elizabeth Islands, at the mouth of Buzzards Bay, where the dear old Commonwealth of Massachusetts is establishing a leper hospital to-day. Put that on record because it is our way of acting on the Sermon on the Mount, and showing that we build upon a rock. And on the Island of Cuttyhunk, the most southerly of the Elizabeth Islands, Gosnold

HENRY WRIOTHESLEY, THIRD EARL OF SOUTHAMPTON.

and his men established the first colony on the North Atlantic shore of the United States. Raleigh had tried before him, on Roanoke Island, where Virginia Dare was born.

I think Gosnold's colony lasted seven weeks. The ruins of the storehouse are there to this day, with the monument which tells the tale. If you want to read the history, take down the "Tempest" and read of Caliban and mussels in the brooks and sassafras logs and seamews and quarrels between sailors and gentlemen. That is exactly the story of what happened in Gosnold's seven weeks.

And at the end of the seven weeks, no one would stay there, and they all went back to London. And they hustled up to the Earl of Southampton's palace and told their story of quarrel, of tempest, of seamews, and of logs.

And according to me, one William Shakespeare, who was the friend and companion of the Earl of Southampton, used to sit in the great hall of the palace and hear these stories. And according to me he was writing the "Tempest" then and brought these stories in. So is it that the *mise en scène* of the "Tempest" is not that of the West Indies or of Bermuda where there are no brooks, nor flying squirrels, nor mussels in the brook nor sassafras logs, but is a copy of Cuttyhunk, as Gosnold and his sailors found it. So is it that Miranda, God bless her! is a Massachusetts girl.

Probably no one in the world accepts this criticism on Shakespeare excepting me. But I do accept it, and this reader had better accept it, for it will be the received comment in the year 1950.

It has been said already in these papers that if you want to know anything, you had better go and see it yourself. That is their text. Personal presence moves the world, as my dear old friend Eli Thayer either said or did not say. I have always referred the remark to him because he lived up to its principle. This is true, that you remember what you have seen as you do not remember so well what you hear, as I think Horace says before me.

So it is that I shall find myself advising this gentle reader to see Massachusetts as I have seen it. It is as a spider living on the hub of his wheel adventures out upon this spoke, upon that, or upon another. Here am I, born on the slope of Beacon Hill, if you please; or as old writers would have said, "as the roadway goes down from Sherburne's to the water." Now just above the place where I was born, not half a quarter of a mile away, is the State House of Massachusetts with a gold pineapple upon the top. This is what Dr. Holmes audaciously called the "hub of the Universe," and the Boston people to this hour chuckle because he said it, thinking in their own hearts, dear souls, that it is true.

What is curious is that by great good fortune the Capitol of Massachusetts is so placed that within five miles of this pineapple is the statistical centre, census after census, of the population of the state. There are so many more people in those great manufacturing towns which have to keep in close touch with the seaboard that when the statistical people do their best to find a mathematical centre for all these hundreds of thousands, it proves that the State House has put itself within a few miles of that centre.

For me, since in this chapter I am to talk more or less about myself, birth in Boston meant radiation in one direction or another. My father saw very soon that the great canal system of New York and the states to the south and westward could not be made to work in New England, though many people thought it could. He "caught on" to the railway system invented in England, and while people thought he was crazy, he foresaw lines of it in his own state. It must have been in 1826 that, as I sat, a little boy four years old, on a little yellow box provided for me in his "chaise," he took my mother out with her little boy sitting thus at their feet, and we came to

QUINCY RAILWAY PITCHER.
(See List of Illustrations.)

the line of the Quincy Railway, the first railway built in the United States. He gave her the reins; he alighted from the chaise; he struck the flat iron rail with his foot to see how closely it was spiked on the timber below; he returned into the chaise and explained to me what the railway was. This is one of the first memories of my life.

THE STOURBRIDGE LION, THE FIRST LOCOMOTIVE IN AMERICA (1829).

From that time nearly to his death problems of engineering occupied him as they referred to railroads or to water supply. When I write my successful novel, and *The Outlook* relieves its bank account by sending me a check for half a year's royalties, I am going to ask Macmonnies to make an equestrian statue of my father with his binocular in his hand. This statue is to be placed without other pedestal on a rock which is half porphyry, in

Wellesley, Massachusetts. For this rock parts the Boston and Worcester Railroad, which he built, from the great Cochituate water-pipes, which he laid there to give life to Boston.

As the surveys for the railroad began, and as they went westward, I and my older brother

THE VEAZIE RAILROAD, BANGOR, MAINE (1836).

Nathan, who explained all things in life to me, were apt to be out with the parties of engineers anywhere between Boston and Worcester. Among other things, those years meant for us and my two sisters that we used to color maps of eastern Massachusetts so that the townships might be clearly distinguished.

In that household we were a unit; where one

went all went, and so the year I was four years old we all went down to Cape Cod. A year or two afterwards, in a great open barouche, we all circumnavigated Cape Ann, Fullum driving with the assistance of myself and my brother. One of those hot summers we went on the canal-boat *General Sullivan* to Lowell, taking only a day for the journey, which now requires forty-five minutes. On that day I saw my first tadpole, and my mother put him into her thimble. Joy of joys, in just such a barouche, as soon as the school vacation came round, every year if possible, we were all taken to the family altar at Westhampton, where my father was born, a journey of nearly three days, the route varying as he liked to trace one valley or another. So soon as railroads were built of course we went everywhere upon them. And so it is that when I read the other day that a man had been in every township of Massachusetts, I wondered why even I had not been in every township of Massachusetts, not on a bicycle, as he went, but mostly in these earlier expeditions.

I first settled down in life in Worcester, which with good reason calls itself the heart of the Commonwealth. The seal of the city is a heart,

Jonathan Edwards.

because the people there are fond of this name. Now Worcester is another excellent radiating point. You can take your friend in your buggy early in an afternoon, and you can cross waters which flow into the Merrimac on the north, into Narragansett Bay and the Thames River on the

JOHN ADAMS.

south, into the Connecticut on the west, and return to your Worcester home before supper.

The old township system of New England holds. There is great pride in almost every one of these little commonwealths, more than three hundred in number. They have great pride in their locality. No one can do them more good than by nursing this pride and trying to make it eternal. Go to Westboro, and they will tell you that Eli Whitney was born here, who revolutionized the industries of America. Go to Northampton, where they will tell you that Jonathan Edwards preached there, and will or will not tell you that they turned him out. Just now twelve hundred young women make their home at Smith College there. Go to Springfield, and you will hear that Springfield is the place where our National Government revolutionized for the world the business of the manufacture of small arms. Go to Quincy, and, besides the railway referred to above, they will show you the birthplace of John Adams, who practically wrote the constitutions of almost all the old Thirteen States. His home was called Braintree then. Go to Amesbury; it was Whittier's home. Go down the river to Byfield, and here was the first woollen manufactory in America. Go to Cambridge, and you

THE BATTLE OF LEXINGTON.

see the statue of the first printer. Go to Williamstown, and here was Mark Hopkins's slab throne, as Garfield described it, and here was a celebrated haycock. Go to Easton; they will tell you that their axes are in the hands of men blacker than any you ever saw, under the equator in Africa. Go to Nantucket, and they say that Burke was talking about them when he told the House of Commons whom he envied. Go to Sheffield, and they say Orville Dewey was born here. Go to Pittsfield, and they say Henry Dawes lived here. Go to Sturbridge, and they say here was the first mine wrought in the United States, which has been kept in operation until now. Go to Gloucester, and they say Massachusetts pays for all her breadstuffs with the fish she draws out of the sea. Plymouth, Concord, Lexington, Bunker Hill — Mr. Webster says the world knows the history by heart. Go to Worcester, and they will tell you where Senator Hoar lived. Go to Wrentham, Helen Keller lives there. Go to Natick, or Newton, and in each of those towns people will tell you that

John Eliot first preached to the Indians there. Go to Marshfield, and it is where Daniel Webster lived and died. Go to Beverly, here was

JOHN ELIOT PREACHING TO THE INDIANS.

the first cotton manufacture in America. Go to Newburyport, John Lowell lived here, the great Emancipator. Go to Concord, and hear about Emerson and Hawthorne. And so on and so on, with hundreds of other places and men.

I have just named Smith College with its twelve hundred pupils. Whoever is thoroughly interested in the education of women ought to visit Smith College in Northampton, to cross the river and to see Mount Holyoke College in Hadley, of which the Campus, if one is to call it so, is really matchless. Take care also that you see Wellesley College, under Miss Hazard, at Wellesley.

I have already named Williams College, which has done and is doing and will do so much for the highest education of young men. When Amherst College was born, now the better part of a century ago, I think there was supposed to be some antagonism in the rivalry between this new broom and the older college in Berkshire. But it is apparent long ago that the founders builded better than they knew, and that there is ample room for them both, even though Dartmouth College is not so far away. The truth is that the country is beginning to find out that the higher education is in no sort what the French call it, secondary education. And happily the more and better we provide, the number of students who mean to profit by this advantage increases in a larger proportion.

RALPH WALDO EMERSON.

But when you speak of colleges, I like to put in this little bit of statistics. I was in a great central high school building of one of our manufacturing towns a year or two ago, and I said to the superintendent of education there that when I was in college at Cambridge, Harvard College had no building which would compare with that. He told me that thirteen of the cities of Massachusetts had provided for their public school service buildings which would quite equal that in which we stood. There are eleven Normal Schools maintained by the state in different sections, several of which would once have ranked as colleges in any of the standards which are familiar to the country.

Now let us recollect all along, this charming local pride. It is the best thing in Massachusetts, and you want to find it wherever you can. Here are more good instances of it. In the beginning, the town of Paxton, up in the Worcester hills, held a town meeting in which they declared war against King George. And if, at this moment, the town of Reading chooses to say that the Widow Dorcas in her home shall have better water than the President has in the White House, and that her sitting-room shall be better lighted at Christmas than this room in which I write, why, the town of Reading lays the pipes and the town of Reading makes the electricity, and asks the permission or the help of nobody this

DESTRUCTION OF TEA IN BOSTON HARBOR.
"Boston Harbor a tea pot to-night! Hurrah for Griffin's Wharf!"

side of Our Father, with whom she works in such exigencies.

When I went to school, the custom in teaching geography was to begin with the Arctic Regions of America, and work slowly down with the vague hope that some day you would arrive at New Zealand as a sort of Z at the end of the world.

Paul Revere.
From the portrait by Gilbert Stuart.

But in practice, what with change of masters and of text-books, you were forever beginning with Greenland, reading about the sea seen by Mackenzie and the seas seen by Mr. Hearne, and probably never travelled far beyond the United States. For me I never studied at school any geography of Asia or of Africa, and I will say in a whisper that it has made no difference whether I ever did or did not. But we did advance in my boyhood so far as to be taught that Massachusetts was "celebrated for its fisheries, and for the part she had in the Revolution." It was also stated that the climate was good, but that "in the spring easterly winds arise which are very disagreeable." These facts, and no others, I think, were impressed upon the youthful mind. It is interesting to me to remember that I never heard an east wind spoken of till, at the age of eleven, I had to learn this sentence, and I asked at home if this were true. So indifferent are little children to their surroundings.

I was twenty-three years old before I ever saw a wheat-field. Of course I had never seen cotton-fields or rice-fields or sugar plantations. But in college I had made long tramps north, west, and east in studying the flora of Middlesex and Essex counties, and a healthy interest in botany, instilled by my dear mother when I was very young, had given a half-scientific interest to such expeditions. At the end of my freshman year I and my brother took a long expedition on foot to see for ourselves the locality of the curious Lancaster or Berlin macle, a crystal, it would be called, which exists in Berlin and Lancaster and nowhere else in the world. From that hour to this I have been telling my young friends that the true way to travel is to travel on foot. Next best to this is a horseback ride; next to this is a journey on a canal. It is only far down in the scale that you come to carriages and stage-coaches, and to bicycles ; and automobiles let us hope never. Wise Elizabeth says that we do not take an automobile because "our object is not to get to this place or that place, but to see what happens as we go."

I was very much laughed at among my near

Christ Church, Salem Street.

friends a generation ago for saying, in a little guide book which I wrote for New England travellers, that the best way to go from Providence to Newport is by a voyage in a friend's yacht. I still hold to that instruction, though it may

THE EVACUATION OF BOSTON, MARCH 17, 1776.
From an engraving by F. T. Stuart of the drawing by L. Hollis.

give one a slightly exaggerated sense of the resources of the country. Thus, the first time I ever went along Cape Cod, my cosmopolitan friend, Mr. Freeman Cobb, took me with his four-in-hand barouche over the admirable highroads of Brewster. We were deprived by accident of the company of a very distinguished French traveller who was "doing" America. And I have delighted myself ever since with imagining what his description of Cape Cod would have been if he had gone with us on that day's outing. For I am afraid from that time to this time no four-in-hand has been driven over those sands, certainly none by a more accomplished or agreeable guide.

Of course the gentle reader may begin where he likes. I should not be sorry if, hiring a cottage at Nahant or Marblehead Neck or on the Beverly Shore, quite early in June, he made William and Edward, if those were the names of his grooms-men, keep up the horses in good condition till Thanksgiving time, and from these centres if he and Madam and the older children made excursions, a week at a time, into the different regions of Massachusetts. But possibly the horses may be sick with some epizoötic disease — possibly William and Edward may have returned for the summer to visit Tipperary or Rügen, and we may need the trolley, steamboat, or, best of all, our good feet. In that case, Boston

THE CONSTITUTION.
From the painting by Marshall Johnson.

is still the best centre. It is an excellent watering-place. There is my own treatise on Picturesque Massachusetts, and my "Historical Boston" and "Harry and Lucy," which might lie on the table. And if it were only a trolley, there are trolley rides by which this reader may sweep what is well-nigh a circle of fifty miles' radius. For Massachusetts Bay, which takes in a segment of perhaps a quarter of this circle, we will rely on the *Othniel* or *Jathniel* or any other of the steam yachts of our friends, or, in a more democratic fashion, we will rely on the daily excursion steamer. For a last resort, at least we can invest five cents in a street-car, and go to the South Boston public baths or to Governor's Island.

You may cut out the list of towns already given, and go to each and all. But to try geographical order, what we really want to see, ranging from north to south, are, first, the towns north of the Merrimac to which we owe the name, now national, of the "Gerrymander." Under Governor Gerry's reign in 1811 this string of towns made the neck of the monster Gerrymander who has gobbled up so many majorities in all parts of many countries between that time and this. I was pleased to see that the name of "Gerrymander" has worked its way into English politics.

THE GERRYMANDER.
(See List of Illustrations.)

In the town of Newburyport, at the mouth of the river, the fighting frigates of the Revolution were built. Think of their names, — the *Marino Faliero*, the *Protector*, the *Tyrannicide*, the *Oliver*

HARVARD COLLEGE IN 1836. THE SECOND CENTENNIAL CELEBRATION.

Cromwell. We knew something of history then. And you must see the river. Take care to take the steamer at Haverhill some day and spend one of the pleasantest days of your life in sailing down the Merrimac to Newburyport. You will have an intelligent captain who will tell you of everything from the eagles in the sky to the shad in the river: the first woollen manufactory, the first cotton manufactory, first caterpillar bridge, first Bill of Rights, origin of the Longfellows, — if anybody cares, of the Hales, certainly of the Lowells and the Parsonses and all the rest of the Essex Junto, if anybody cares for history. If you believe that the manufacture of cotton is the one great object for which God made the world, as the old Economists seemed to think, go to Lowell and Lawrence, and delight in the conversation of those very spirited and intelligent manufacturers. Or is it wars and rumors of wars? Go to Lexington and Concord, or see at Salem where the first blood of the Revolution was drawn, or at Arlington, where a black man commanded a company of exempts to whom we owe our first victory. Or

Charlestown, where is the United States Navy Yard with its enormous dry dock. Give a day to Marblehead, where you can still find some old salts who will talk to you of the *Constitution*, or you might go down to the North End Park in Boston and board her.

Harvard College? You have heard, perhaps, of that. Go and see it; tell them, you read in *The Outlook* that there was such a place, and you thought you would like to compare it with your own college at New Padua. You could not spend a week more pleasantly than I spent one once on the Great Brewster Island. The rest of the world knew that Napoleon III was a prisoner of state thirty-six hours before I did. But I do not see but that I am as happy now as I was then for all that.

Do you want to see them build ironclads? Go to Fore River. Or will you shed tears over the first winter in Plymouth? Shed them at the burying-place, which is very like what it was then. Is it ropes and cordage? Take a trolley from the burial-place and learn all about that, — or where I fired my first gun? Sandwich.

Henry W. Longfellow

Recollect now, if you please, that you have come into the Old Colony — three counties, Plymouth, Bristol, and Barnstable. And in those counties, from the time when old John Robinson said, "There is more light and more truth yet

DEPARTURE OF THE PILGRIM FATHERS FROM DELFT HAVEN.
From the painting by Charles W. Cope.

to come out of God's Holy Word," there has been more freedom in religion — let one say, reverently, more persons have enjoyed easy access from the child to our Father who is in heaven — than in any other region of the same population in this world into which His kingdom is to come.

In saying this, I hope the imaginary student whom I am leading will spend enough time on Cape Cod. The last time I visited its capital, Barnstable, I asked my wife if she had ever gone into a jail. It proved that she never had, and I took her into the jail of this county — what in New England we call the County House, because it is both jail and house of correction and the residence of the keeper. We had the pleasure of seeing the accomplished keeper and his friendly wife and the cells of the jail, but there were no prisoners there. I tried afterwards to make the clergyman of the place (he would be called bishop if ours were an effete civilization) describe the social influences which led to such a result. But he said the thing was a matter of course — there could be no interest in any such discussion. He said I had better write the book myself, which I have never had time to do.

In our day you can take an excellent train to Provincetown, and you can stop and see the cranberry plantations which have proved even more profitable than the old deep-sea fisheries of the

Cape. You may hear traditions upon traditions of the wreck of the *Quidah* pirate and of the *Somerset* man-of-war. You will find a little odd

EDWARD WINSLOW.

remnant of the recollections of the fisheries and privateering. You will come back glad that you have been to Cape Cod, and sorry that you cannot stay there longer.

Another good centre would be Worcester, "the heart of the Commonwealth," as I said just now. An Englishman named Samuel Slater, in what is now Pawtucket in Rhode Island, really established the cotton manufacture of

Public Worship at Plymouth by the Pilgrims.

America. In time the Cabots were before him at Beverly. Slater came up to Worcester one day, it must have been in the thirties of the last century, and young Pliny Merrick said to him, "We shall never have any large factories in Worcester, because we have but little water-power here." Mr. Slater replied: "Mr. Merrick, you will live to see the day when Worcester needs ali the water in its Mill Brook to feed the steam-engines which will be running in this valley." His prophecy was long since true, for they had to build the great reservoir up in their hills to feed their steam-engines, the locomotives among the rest.

I have said twenty times in print and elsewhere that Worcester, which was once my home, is a Western town in the heart of New England; and this is still true. Here are the old New England dignities, even conventionalities and etiquettes, and here is the "run-with-the-machine" and "get-out-of-the-way-boy" of a great Western city. I do not think they know themselves how many nationalities are here. I do not say how many Swedish churches there are, because they will build another while I am reading the proof. Armenians? Yes! French Canadians? Oh, yes, of course. And so on and so on. But still the old sturdy Worcester of Isaiah Thomas, when after the battle of Lexington he put his printing-press and his types into wagons in Boston, and, arriving three or four days after, printed the Massachusetts *Spy* in Worcester, which he and his have printed from that day to this year. Ah! there were many of the antislavery years

THE WAYSIDE INN, SUDBURY, MASS.
(Present Day.)

when the *Spy* was as another gospel to these Worcester County farmers.

The reader must let me stop, for another minute, to tell how the town came to be named Worcester. Governor Andros, whom we all hated because he was James the Second's man, had to order a session of the General Court of Massachusetts. So they came together and they meant to do something before he prorogued them, as they knew he would do. What would be a good thing to do? Why, here is a petition from some settlers by Lake Quinsigamond who want to be made a township. Yes, we will charter them. And so we will show King James that we can create a town. And what shall we name the town? We will name it Worcester, because with

SENATOR HOAR.

Worcester in England Charles II got his worst thrashing, and ran away as fast as his horse would carry him, for his exile of nine years. Let him put that in his pipe and smoke it. There is a good deal of that sort of Worcester left. It is to

Worcester that Carroll Wright has been called to manage the academic college in Clark University, which Stanley Hall launched and directs. Mr. Salisbury, one of Worcester's public-spirited citizens, died a few months ago. He has by the princely bequests in his will given a firm foundation to what will be one of the finest galleries of painting and sculpture in the country. And from Worcester, if you look at any map of that county, you will see that there extend six spider-webs of railroads, which will take you anywhere. It is the Worcester from which dear Senator Hoar started whenever he went to Washington.

When I lived in Worcester, we used to laugh about the street corner below Brinley Hall. We used to say that if the Chief Justice of the United States died, a few of the Worcester men would get together on that corner and determine who was his proper successor from the leaders of the County Bar. Dr. Samuel Haven, one of our modest students of history, used to have his joke in saying that Timothy Ruggles, of Worcester County, would

THE "COLUMBIA" AND THE "LADY WASHINGTON" ON THE PACIFIC COAST.
From original drawing in possession of Mrs. A. S. Twombly, a granddaughter of Captain Gray.

have been the proper military chief in the Revolution if by misfortune he had not been a Tory attached to King George. We took Artemas Ward of Shrewsbury.

To this hour those Worcester County people have a fashion of thinking a good deal for themselves. It was my business in 1888, analyzing the vote of Worcester County after the election of the younger Harrison, to find, to the confusion of people who distrust universal suffrage and think we ought to have a property qualification, and all that "you know," the somewhat interesting fact that there were more landholders in the territorial boundary of the city of Worcester than there were voters in that critical election. A young fellow walks into a bank parlor in Worcester, shows them his new invention in wood or in horsehair, in wool, in ivory, in steel, or in copper, and the Worcester banker sees that the young fellow does not drink, nor play cards, nor swear, and he gives him a discount because he was born in Worcester County. And then the young fellow goes away, and before you have done with him, he is in business correspondence with the Sultan of some unexplored region in Central Africa. This was the Worcester of my time, and I fancy it is the Worcester of to-day. In my time there was not a manufacturing corporation in the city. Every man made his own invention, took out his own patent, drove his own steam-engine, and made his own fortune.

HENRY LAURENS DAWES.

Another charming centre is farther west at Pittsfield. Here, again, two lines of railway cross each other. Here are some of the most intelligent and charming people in the world. And here they have been since the place was called Wendellboro, and Dr. Holmes's ancestors lived here. You may go north to Greylock, determined to send your son to Williams College; you may go south down the valley of the Housatonic, and make a call on Asaph Hall, the great astronomer, as he lives among the shadows of

Henry D. Thoreau.

the hills. Here lived and here died our honored friend Henry Laurens Dawes, who maintained the good name of Massachusetts so long in the Senate at Washington. Here was one man who understood the Indian problem, and while he held the reins nobody talked of dishonor in our dealings with the Indians. The story is told of Charles Sumner that he said of supposed corruption in Washington that nobody had ever approached him with a dishonorable proposal. We Massachusetts people boast that from his day to our day that story could be applied to either of our Senators. Just before he died Mr. Dawes had delivered a few lectures at Dartmouth College, and perhaps Williams College, on matters connected with government. What a pity that he could not have lived for a generation more, if it were only to give us such results of his experience!

I will not send this sheet away till I have said to any young traveller that I have found it a good practice wherever I journey to see the people who make the laws of a country. I never go to London but I ask them at our Legation to give me what passes they can into the gallery of the

CHARLES SUMNER.
From a photograph in possession of F. J. Garrison, Esq.

House of Commons, and I sit there night after night to see how England is governed. In the same way I have sat hours in the gallery of the Chambers at Paris and in the elegant gallery of the Parliament of Spain. In travelling in America I always try to go into the state Capitol, wherever it is, and see their methods. You get a great deal more than mere information as to legislative customs and laws; you see a great deal of the character of the people. So this I say to the intelligent traveller, that in either of these states of which I have been speaking he may get good lessons for himself, be he President, Judge, Senator, or sixteenth assistant in an Auditor's office at Washington, if he will go into the gallery of either state legislature and see with what dignity and promptness these legislators address themselves to their duties. Just now I am reading Gladstone, to see with amazement how well the English Parliament goes on in the hands of five or six hundred gentlemen in England who take upon themselves the direction of that empire. And I lay down that book with a certain American pride, that when you send two or three hundred men to the state legislature for a few months, taking them from mill, forge, fishing-boat, counting-room, pulpit, garden, farm, quarry, or whatever other range of life you choose, when you follow them to the House of Representatives or to the Senate of their state, the whole machinery of legislation moves forward with absolute dignity, as if each man were trained in hereditary succession to make laws for his people. So, indeed, each man is, if he have the good luck to be born in New England.

Professor Asa Gray.

How does Massachusetts show in the Hall of Fame? By hook or by crook, we succeeded, a fair majority of us, in selecting twenty-nine names for Miss Gould's list of heroes. They were to be the names of Americans by birth who had died more than ten years before our selection. Well, out of the twenty-nine, Massachusetts had fifteen, if you will let us count in Channing, Daniel Webster, Beecher, and Asa Gray. This includes Longfellow who was born in Maine when it was a part of Massachusetts.

She had John Adams, Benjamin Franklin, Daniel Webster, Joseph Story, George Peabody, Eli Whitney, Samuel F. B. Morse, Asa Gray, Jonathan Edwards, Horace Mann, Henry Ward Beecher, Ralph Waldo Emerson, Nathaniel Hawthorne, Henry Longfellow, William Ellery Channing.

In the picture gallery of Harvard College we have three Presidents, — John Adams, John Quincy Adams, and Rutherford B. Hayes, because he was at our Law School. Hayes was born and educated in boyhood in Ohio. Still, these will do for our fame in the hall where for one reason or another we could not include John Hancock, Samuel Adams, Edward Everett, Wendell Phillips, William Lloyd Garrison, Henry Laurens Dawes, and George Frisbie Hoar. Hall of Fame or not, they are dear to us.

CHAPTER VI

RHODE ISLAND

THE Island of Rhode Island is in Narragansett Bay. Fashion is not a fool, and fashion in America has selected the Island of Rhode Island as the best place to live in for six months of the year. From this beautiful island the "State of Rhode Island and Providence Plantations" is named. "Little Rhody," it is affectionately called by its inhabitants. The books will tell you that Rhode Island was named by its discoverer, Adrian Block, from the island of Rhodes in the Ægean Sea. But the books give no reason, nor does anybody give any reason, why Adrian Block should have named the island which he discovered after the Ægean; nobody knows that he ever was in the Ægean.

According to me, when Block swept into Narragansett Bay he found a splendid grove of rhododendron. If you wish to be accurate, this was the rhododendron maximum of Gray and the modern botanists. It is the finest flower in the

OCHRE POINT, NEWPORT.

"Fashion in America has selected the Island of Rhode Island as the best place to live in for six months of the year."

American flora. Adrian Block saw it then for the first time.

> Hard a port! Now close to shore sail!
> Starboard now, and drop your foresail!
> See, boys, what yon bay discloses,
> What yon open bay discloses!
> Where the breeze so gently blows is
> Heaven's own land of ruddy roses.

> Past the Cormorant we sail,
> Past the rippling Beaver Tail.
> Green with summer, red with flowers,
> Green with summer, fresh with showers,
> Sweet with song and red with flowers,
> Is this new-found land of ours!
>
> Roses close above the sand,
> Roses on the trees on land,
> I shall take this land for my land,
> Rosy beach and rosy highland,
> And I name it Roses Island.

According to me, Block named the island Roses Island when he saw this magnificent spectacle. If you will come and see me where I write, not far away, and come before July is over, I will take you into a rhododendron covert, where you may see the same thing. So far as I know, no one excepting the immediate circle of my dearest friends believes in this interpretation or etymology. But it is within this generation that I published it to the world, and we will still hope that it will gradually reach its place at the head of the theories about the name of Rhode Island. (Since I put this statement into print an attentive correspondent tells me that Roger Williams says in one of his letters that the island was named from the roses on its shores.)

As I have said already, the best way to go to

Jean Baptiste Donatien de Vimeure, Comte de Rochambeau.
1725—1807.

Newport is to go in a friend's yacht from Providence. The voyage may take you a longer or shorter time, according as the yacht has steam power or has not; according as winds are north or south. But you will not care much for that.

It will be a pleasant voyage, anyway. So pleasant is it that you will not be far amiss if, going to New York from Boston, you go as your grandfather used to do — in a steamboat from Providence. It is not so large as the Fall River steamboat, but it gives you this charming bay. Every inch of that has its story, if you should happen to find some old sachem who can tell you that story. "Story? God bless you!" Yes. Stories of Roger Williams, of Canonicus and Canonchet, of Wampum (ask William Weeden to tell you that); stories of King Philip, and of Tower Hill, and of the Narragansett fight; stories of the capture of the *Gaspée;* stories of the capture of Prescott; stories of Rochambeau, of Chastellux, of Lafayette and a hundred brave Frenchmen; stories of a thousand pretty girls

CHEVALIER DE CHASTELLUX.

whom they danced and flirted with; stories of the slave trade, of the De Wolfs and the Hoppers and the Herreshoffs; stories of clambake — stories enough even if the voyage should last from June to October. And by the time you come to the

"DESTRUCTION OF THE SCHOONER 'GASPÉE' IN THE WATERS OF RHODE ISLAND, 1772."
From an old engraving.

rough turning of Point Judith you will be asleep in your stateroom and the rough sea will not trouble you.

Point Judith?—Just a word about Point Judith. Dear old John Hull, the same who coined the first silver money for Massachusetts and showed to

Cromwell and King Charles and the sachems of New England that Massachusetts had the sovereign rights of coining money — this same John Hull had a daughter Judith. If you are well up in your Hawthorne, you know that the night Samuel Sewall (afterwards Chief Justice, the same who hanged the witches) married Judith Hull, old John Hull, her father, put her into one scale of the balance and poured pine-tree shillings into the other enough to weigh her down. One hundred and twenty-five pounds sterling the girl weighed, if you will trust me who have read the same in the manuscript ledger of her new husband. This, according to Hawthorne, was her dower.

Well, this same John Hull and his sometime son-in-law Sewall went into a fine speculation in the southern part of Rhode Island, and bought the Petaquamscot Purchase from the Indians of their day. If you care, dear reader, it is in my own house in the Petaquamscot Purchase overlooking Point Judith, when I look out of the window, that I am dictating these words.

Well, dear old John Hull, whose grandchildren's great-grandchildren came in here just now with the Providence *Journal*, wanted to give to this outlying point a name, and he gave it Judith Hull's name, I think, before she was Judith Sewall. One of my New Hampshire correspondents, sniffing at the ocean and all it brings with it, asks me if he named Judith Hull from Point Judith; if she were misty and frigid and stormy and disagreeable in general, and if it were fair that he should borrow the name from the storm-washed point for the baby who was to be, as it proved, the ancestor of heroes. Dr. Holmes's Dorothy Q, for instance, is in that line. But the New Hampshire

SAMUEL SEWALL.
From an old engraving.

correspondent is all wrong. Judith Hull was not named from Point Judith; Point Judith was named from Judith Hull.

And while we are gossiping about the first Petaquamscot Purchase I may as well say that some of the Narragansett Indians took Roger Williams to what we call here "Sugar Loaf Hill" and bade him survey the prospect. One is reminded of the "exceeding high mountain" of another story. They told Roger Williams, who seems to have believed it, that some of their ancestors went from Petaquamscot to the regions of the Blue Hills in Massachusetts. And they gave Roger Williams to understand that when the Massachusetts people exiled him to the Narragansett country he came back to the centre of New England civilization, which lay around these waters of what we call "Salt Pond." What I know is that when Judge Sewall died, he and his wife Hannah left a farm of five hundred acres here at Petaquamscot to Harvard College, and the college still uses the income towards the "support and education of youths at college, especially such as shall be sent from Petaquamscot aforesaid, English or Indian, if any such there be." So we are trying to repay Judith's debts. Hannah, if anybody cares, was the successor of Judith.

Roger Williams soon found, I think, that the

LANDING OF ROGER WILLIAMS.
From an old engraving.

Puritan oligarchs of Massachusetts Bay had "kicked him upstairs," as our English friends say. He wrote to somebody that in our Rhode Island country he had seen at one time strawberries enough in fruit to load a ship with. Indeed, it is in this same letter that we have the famous epigram of his friend Dr. Boteler, that

God might have made a better berry, but that He never did. Whoever is bragging about our Continent to an effete Europe may like to say that the introduction of the American strawberry into the gardens of the old world resulted in a manifold and manifest improvement of the strawberry of to-day over the strawberry of Virgil and Pliny.

Dear Roger Williams, he went and came in this region, he traversed our beautiful lakes in his canoe, and he learned the language of Canonicus and the rest, and preserved it for posterity. He has left us one and another of sidelights on his time which interpret to us his own good sense and religious philosophy.

I am fond of saying that I like to live in New England and that I like to live in the South; that Providence has, therefore, chosen for me this summer home of mine as far south as one can go and stay in New England all the time. This is certain, that our poor scattered Algonquins, be they Penacooks or Mystics or Naticks or Abernakis or Aberginians, as they froze in our average New England temperature of forty-three degrees, felt their blood run faster and life more beautiful when a south wind blew in upon them. So in their imaginative mood they fancied that heaven was in the southwest. They thought they were nearer heaven in Rhode Island than they were on the slopes of the White Mountains. If they could keep in the open air here more than they could there, they were right in this conception.

ROGER WILLIAMS.
Statue by Franklin Simmons, at Providence, R. I.

Whatever the legend of "Sugar Loaf Hill" may be worth, there is no doubt that the Narragansetts, who made this region their home, were the superiors in government, in commerce, in language, in the whole range of savage civilization, of all the New England Indians.

Williams liked them and they liked him, and for nearly fifty years his relations with their leaders proved to be of great value to the infant confederacy of New England. According to me, his studies of the Indian character with his studies of the Indian language are the most important documents of that time which we have left in our too scanty ethnological libraries.

Do not neglect by any means to go to Bristol — quaint, old-fashioned, historical, and beautiful. You see there were days when the maritime commerce of Bristol was, I think, quite equal to that of New York; certainly it was in advance over that of Boston. To hold the Narragansett Bay was the ambition of the English commanders through the Revolution. And there is many a Revolutionary story, now of battle, now of adventure, now of intrigue, of these waters, and of these shores. Look on the right pane of the right window and you shall find where some modest patriot wrote on the glass what he seems not to have dared to say to the face of "the incomparable Miss Abby Brown."

Captain Esek Hopkins,
"Commandant en Chef la Flotte Américaine."

It was the Bristol slave traders whom Mr. Webster rebuked in his Plymouth address of 1820. 1808 marked the year when the slave trade was prohibited almost of course by Congress. But the shackles were still forged in Bristol County in Massachusetts, and the shackles went from Bristol in Rhode Island to the West African shore.

The yachtsmen still exult in the name of Herreshoff, and in the fame which Bristol has won when she has sent out such boats as the *Columbia* and the *Defender* and the other champions of the sea. Whoever wants to see one of the finest memorials of the finest old life of New England must obtain an introduction which shall open to him the doors of the Herreshoff homesteads.

Bristol does not send shackles to Africa any longer; but very likely, my dear Annabel, when you walk across the snowy sidewalk next December, you will be wearing Bristol overshoes. I do not mean to intimate that they are too small for those pretty feet.

I think the audacity of the Rhode Islanders in their early conflict with the English navy on one point and another of Narragansett Bay gives them the highest place in the chronological history of our independence. Our first Admiral Hopkins was a Rhode Islander. When he stole the powder from Bermuda and the Bahamas and sent it up to poor Washington at Cambridge, he did the right thing at the right time. Paul Jones never can say too much of his Narragansett seamen. In those days, indeed, Rhode Island supplied the West Indies with what they wanted to eat and with the horses which the Islanders rode upon. We have changed all that, for horses and wheat now go from another valley nearer the West Indies and far away from New England.

But in those days Berkeley, resting as he made the preparations for the great American College at Bermuda, gave Newport its first fame among men and women of letters. And he is remembered here as I suppose he is not remembered anywhere else but in California. "Westward the star of empire takes its way." The reader will remember that Dartmouth College is the child of Wheelock, who was a beneficiary under Berkeley's bequest to Yale College. I have no Rhode Island excursion which pleases me more than my visit to the Berkeley Museum which the Colonial Dames have established in Berkeley's old home at Newport. A good portrait of Berkeley is among the treasures at Yale College in New Haven, where Berkeley made himself a real friend. "The Minute Philosophy" and others of the really scientific philosophical books — Mrs. Eddy would say prophetical books — were thought out in Berkeley's walks at Newport. I have fancied that the freshness of the sea breeze and the tonic of the surf might be traced in them to this day.

Something — and the reader must tell me what — has given to the State of Rhode Island and Providence Plantations a race of Idealists, such as is hard to parallel elsewhere in a period so short as the time since Roger Williams landed at Mosshassuck. Here is Williams himself, with all his claims to being the earliest prophet of real freedom of conscience. Here is Berkeley; there are the traditions of George Fox, and the warm welcome which Rhode Island gave him. For here was the one haven of rest for the Quakers in the days before William Penn established for them another. I have worshipped in the Quaker meeting-house which was built in honor of George Fox's first visit here. It must have been that the absolute independence of every man as he approaches his God, not to say of every hamlet as it built its roads or its schoolhouse, had something to do with this vein of mysticism or idealism which runs all through Rhode Island history.

George Fox.

Here was Samuel Hopkins, the preacher, with his protest against the slave trade, when the slave trade was all the fashion in Providence and in

Rhode Island. And here was William Ellery Channing, who remembered his own shudder when as a boy he heard Hopkins describe hell fire with enthusiasm. Here was Rowland Hazard, first of that honored name, who taught us that man is a Creative Force, the first antagonist to Jonathan Edwards worthy of his steel. Here was Jemima Wilkinson, who led to New York the first colony which was tolerated by the savage Iroquois. Here was Alice Rathburn, the charm of whose eloquence is still referred to with love by the old people up and down through the "South County," while no word that she said has been remembered.

Indeed, it is the same individualism which to this hour makes the farmer build his house as far from the next one as possible. It was this same individualism which made Rhode Island the last of the thirteen states to join in the Union. It was not, I think, that her leaders saw any special difficulties in the Federal Constitution. It was rather that they did not want to do what other people do. I am afraid that

that characteristic lingers among some of them to this day.

"George," said a friend of mine to his friend, "I hear thee is drawn on the jury."

"Yes, friend, I am on the jury. It is just in haying time, too!"

"Well, George, thee has only to listen to the other eleven, and agree to what the men of most sense say."

"Agree! Friend, I shall agree with nobody!"

There is Roger Williams in the twentieth century.

Dear Richard Greenough used to say to me that in matters of art Newport was an American Venice. He used to ask me whether we might not manufacture a theory in which south winds off the sea, with those fogs which soften harsh outlines, and that more even temperature which soothes all audacity, shall I say with a sort of dew which belongs to a high revelation half concealed, — he used to say that all this gave to men in the Italian Venice a charm of color, a certain indecision in outline and with it a wealth of fancy and imagination which had made the Venetian school of art. According to Richard, you may trace such influences of climate in the work of Titian, Veronese, of Tintoretto, and the rest, and according to him there is a school of our American younger art which belongs to this

American Venice, a Venice on an island, a Venice where you go about in boats, a Venice where the water plashes against your door-step, and where the south winds blow off the sea. He remembered

GILBERT STUART.

that our dear old Smibert was established here, Copley's teacher. He said that such was the training-place of Malbone, of Gilbert Stuart, and Allston, and, in our later days, of Stagg. And why else had he gone down there to live himself? Where did Hunt go? and where is Miss Jane Hunt to-day? Why else did Mr. Richards make his home as near this Venice as he could? Why else are there so many pictures of the best on the walls of your friends in Providence and Bristol and Newport?

I was talking one day with a very charming Rhode Island lady, who lived in Providence, whose benefactions have made her known to half the world. She said to me, very simply, "Yes, I had rather live in a workshop than in a tradeshop." She meant that she liked to live in a state where everybody you meet makes something. We call it manufacture, but they do not make things by hand any more. They set going a bit of machinery, and the wheels rattle and the pistons slide, while they go off to the tops of the Pyramids or to the South Antarctic to reach the Southern Pole. Somehow or other, more things are made by these five hundred thousand people than are made by so many people anywhere else in the world, so they tell me, and I suppose it is true.

When I go to Byfield as above, they tell me they first made woollen cloth there. I do not know how it is, but in South Kingston, here, they tell me that the first Rowland Hazard was the first person to weave woollen thread by anything like our modern machinery. What I know is that our Peacedale won the Imperial Prize at Paris as being the best-organized town of manufacture in the world. What I know is that there is hardly a waterfall in Rhode Island which is not chained. I remember how a Providence man once said to me that there were twenty villages every Sunday in the broad aisle of the church where he worshipped God.

How does this happen? It happens thus: that the Gulf Stream moves silently and steadily along the shore. It feeds the fogs rising from the ocean and drifting slowly over the mainland. It means that the dew distils from heaven; if only men would remember that it is from heaven that it distils. So when other streams run dry, the ponds in Rhode Island, my pond under my window here, Worden's Pond, two miles west of me, Quidnick Pond, Witchaug Pond, Mahwansecut Pond, are full, while elsewhere men are talking of artificial reservoirs for their water or are shutting down their machinery because no water flows. Rhode Island is the first manufacturing state in the world, they tell me, because the good God of heaven made her ponds in these high lands which are not mountains, and give her steady reservoirs, on which she can draw when the rest of the world is dry. Well, what we call material laws, as I study them, prove to belong in the will of the same God whom I call the Holy Spirit. Anyway, it happens, as we irreverently say, that by the side of Worden's Pond I find there grew up such a man as Corliss, who with one stroke enlarged the power of mankind by fifteen per cent. I wish that I thought mankind were grateful enough to him for the benefaction.

A state of Idealists, you tell me. Yes, and of idealists who know what it is to bring in the kingdom. This is what Mrs. Richmond meant and what her life illustrated. We do not let women file right or file left or hold their muskets two inches from their noses; we do not let them fling themselves against the walls of Peking or Badajos; but such a woman as Mrs. Richmond or Miss Bradley signs a check, after she has taken advice, and then a dam is built across some stream and a turbine goes to work in the water, spinning-frames make thread of cotton or of wool, and the looms weave it into cloth soft enough, if you please, for the cradle of an emperor's baby; and close to the turbine and the waterfall and the spinning-frame and the loom are hundreds of happy homes where the boys grow up to be men and the girls to be women, with the sky blue over their heads, and the fields green out of the windows, and the forests all ready for the children to wander in and be happy in and build their castles of pine needles. I do not wonder that Mrs. Richmond liked to live in her workshop.

We must hurry away. We must go to Connecticut and see how they handle the problems there. But we do not leave Rhode Island without remembering the Browns, and Brown University, and Francis Wayland, who gave that University its fame for half a century. Let

FRANCIS WAYLAND.
"The first educator of his time."

me ask in a parenthesis what is that matchless power by which some board of trustees picks out a young preacher named Francis Wayland "when he began to be about thirty years of age," and places him where he proves to be the first educator of his time? Remember that, ye boards of appointment who have to deal with the nominations of men who are to serve the world "when they began to be about thirty years of age." What Garfield said of Mark Hopkins could have been said of this leader of half a century, that you could make a university if you put Francis Wayland at "one end of a pine slab and his pupil at the other."

Nor let me forget Washington's great second. I asked Jared Sparks once what would have happened if Washington had been killed in any of the fighting around Philadelphia, in 1777, in the Revolution. Sparks said to me that if Nathanaël Greene could have taken his place, all would have been well; that Greene was fit to discharge every duty which Washington discharged. And I think Sparks said that Washington knew this. You know the state of Georgia gave Greene a plantation because he rescued it. And it will not hurt you to remember that on that plantation Eli Whitney invented the cotton-gin and so changed the history of the world.

And when you come to spend your six months in Rhode Island, do not forget to find out Greenwich, which was the home of the Greenes, and spend a night, if you please, at the "Bunch of Grapes." Or go down, if you please, to hear the boys recite their Virgil in Greenwich Academy. And for one more person in Rhode Island, let me remind you of the charming story of John Carter Brown, the millionaire who was willing to be linked with the despised and rejected John Brown of Harper's Ferry.

FORT CONNANICUT, R.I.

CHAPTER VII

CONNECTICUT

EVERY political advance, every sane constitution of government, every crisis, and every step taken for human freedom goes to the maintenance of happy homes. This is George Frisbie Hoar's central statement. For us, the laws of Alfred, Magna Charta, the fight at Naseby, the Bill of Rights, the Declaration of Independence, Constitutional Government the Union of States, all have meant that men should have Happy Homes.

Connecticut has perhaps worked her name into history as the state which is most successful in this business. Compare Switzerland with her in that line, if you choose. Compare Vermont. But Connecticut is older than Vermont, and her history from the beginning has been the history of groups of men who came together in different places, and lived together, and made laws, each community for itself, simply that they might have happy homes — Home Rule. You see, they

CAPTAIN WADSWORTH CONCEALING THE CHARTER OF CONNECTICUT.

have as yet no piling up of people in prison cells called "apartments," nor crowding together in barracks called "tenements" — or they have not many such. I have heard a man say that in their largest city — in New Haven or in Hartford — a man can get more out of life than he can in any other city in the world. I am not sure but this is true.

The "land of steady habits," people used to say; and before they said that they used to make up absurd codes and say that they were the "Blue Laws of Connecticut." These "Blue Law" codes, as they were printed, were fictions; but the fiction itself implies what is true — that in the making of laws in their little assemblies these people always had the fundamental idea of Right. It was not for expediency, it was not for profit, but it was to fulfil the law of the Living God, that the first generation legislated. Well, from such a little state as that large things have followed. The Western Reserve in Ohio was a new Connecticut, where the land was fertile and the winters were not cold, where every seed would bear fruit an hundred fold. And Connecticut may well claim the credit for what the Western Reserve has done: in our own time, for Giddings and Hayes and Garfield and Grant, — I must not say, for the Church of Latter-Day Saints, which I suppose the Western Reserve perhaps would be glad to forget. Mr. Calhoun once said that he remembered a session of the

National House of Representatives when nearly half of the members of the House were graduates of Yale College or natives of Connecticut.

THE CHARTER OAK.

I think the minority of such people was only five less than the majority.

Somewhere in the fifties of the last century a French gentleman called on me who had been sent out from France by Louis Napoleon, or somebody, to study American education. As in duty bound, he had gone first into Canada. He had learned all he could about education in Canada, and then he had been attracted, as La Salle was, to the Valley of the Mississippi, and he had "done" the ancient Louisiana; that is, he had gone through all the states of our Middle West on what people call an "educational" visit. He had reserved New England for the end. And he said to me: "Everywhere I found that the teachers in the American schools, whether of Canada or the Mississippi Valley, are from two provinces — Massachusetts and Connecticut. I said to myself, This is unheard of in history — that all the people in a large nation shall be taught by teachers from two of its smallest subdivisions. And I asked for the statistics for the birth of the teachers, and nobody knew anything about it. But I said, When I come to Connecticut and Massachusetts I can obtain the statistical information on this subject. And now I have come here nobody knows anything about it and nobody cares."

I promised to provide for him some sort of official report on this business, and so I asked a dear old sachem, a near friend of mine, how many of the young people of his particular town, when they left school, began as teachers somewhere

OLIVER ELLSWORTH.
An eminent Connecticut statesman and jurist.

or other. He heard me with some impatience, and then said, "Why, all of them, of course!" This exclamation of his corresponds quite nearly with what at one time was the Southern impression regarding the New England schoolmaster. He was a Connecticut man. In the southern part of the nation there is many an old joke or epigram or anecdote which belongs to the period when a Connecticut Yankee was spoken of as talking through his nose and rolling his R's and "teaching school."

One may say in passing that that abominable expression is pure Yankee, and it is heard nowhere but in the purest Yankee literature.

In our day Connecticut feels, as all the rest of New England feels, the wave of European and Canadian emigration. The old-line rulers of Connecticut, the sons of her own soil who grew up used to home rule, are worried more or less by finding voters who neither know nor care whether they live in Connecticut or in Dakota so far as history goes. They are citizens of the United States, but do not know what the three vines on the seal of Connecticut mean, nor who invented the motto of the state of Connecticut. But, for all that and all that, they retain steadfastly in Connecticut some of the old stand-by habits of home rule. It is worth while to say this if I am writing for people who come from the West

JONATHAN TRUMBULL, GOVERNOR OF CONNECTICUT, 1769–1783.
Said to have been the original "Brother Jonathan."

and South to enjoy the seashore at Watch Hill, at Saybrook, at New Haven, or anywhere on the

Sound. We cannot do enough to awaken local pride by the study of local history in regions which are inhabited by people who have no local pride and know nothing of local history. I have said this whenever I could in public schools and in these papers.

Our newspapers would be a great deal better if some of the people who wrote for them knew more of the traditions, even the language, of five thousand different centres of American life.

Remember, for instance, that in that critical struggle of the Revolution which we like to go back to, there was, strictly speaking, no revolution in Connecticut; every form of government went on without a break of a hair, as it had done before. The elections were the old colonial elections. Governor Trumbull was chosen as every other Governor had been chosen in every other Connecticut election from the beginning. Randolph and some of the other English Governors were commissioned in 1680 as Governors of New England, but they exercised no power in Connecticut except perhaps sending a catch-poll to hunt up a fugitive. When the Revolution came, Connecticut had her Governor and her army; she knew how to commission her officers and to arm her troops. Ethan Allen took Ticonderoga in 1775, and told the commander that he did it in the name of the great Jehovah and the Continental Con-

ETHAN ALLEN AT TICONDEROGA.

gress. This was a very imaginative use of language. The only commission he had was from the state of Connecticut, and she used such power exactly as she had used it in commissioning colonels for one hundred and fifty years.

Chastellux, who was Rochambeau's favorite aide, naturally had many occasions in the Revolution to cross from Newport to the Hudson and eventually to Yorktown and back again. The journey was always, if you will observe, on horseback. Chastellux says early in his book that in all the time when he had been in America he had never seen a man of military age who had not served against King George. This is good testimony as to what Connecticut was. It shows the other side of the appeals we have from Washington to "Brother Jonathan" when he wanted troops of a sudden; and the admirable military records of Connecticut, which have been so well printed and edited, show how Connecticut became ready to answer such appeals. When in 1776 Washington was sure he must fortify New York harbor he sent the Connecticut General Ward, the same who had been at Louisburg, to garrison the city with his Connecticut men. And afterwards it was Knowlton, who was killed within the limits of our Central Park, who led the Connecticut regiment that day of which Washington said in a general order that the behavior of this corps was worthy of any army in any time. My kinsman Hale belonged there, but he was in prison in New York, if indeed he were not already dead.

I forget which of the French gentlemen it is

HARTFORD.
From an old engraving.

who tells that nice story about Greene's early training. Rochambeau, with a great staff, was riding across country when somebody's horse's feet wanted attention. So they stopped at a Connecticut town and sent for a blacksmith. While the blacksmith was at work some one asked Rochambeau what he "did ter hum." Now the truth is that in times of peace a French maréchal of Louis XVI.'s Court did not do much after he had fanned young ladies or offered snuff to princes. But Rochambeau answered that he was a Maréchal de France. Then the curious Yankee followed up his questioning by asking what maréchal meant, and some very bright English-speaking man on the staff answered that maréchal meant blacksmith. This pleased the Yankee. "It's an excellent trade," he said; "it's an excellent trade. Our General Greene is a blacksmith."

I have intimated in another article that if you will go up into northwest Connecticut, into the neighborhood of Canaan Falls, you will find Asaph Hall, the same who discovered the moons of Mars, and he will show you the glories of hills and valleys and waterfalls on this earth. If you will spend a week or two at Norwich — they call it the Rose City — you will find a group of charming people who would never let me name them, and you would have a chance to see how an independent town governs itself and how all the delights of the highest civilization may be found without the clatter and frills of smoke and dust of a great city. In Hartford, as I said, or in New Haven, men say that you can get more out of life in twenty-four hours than you can anywhere else in the world. This is sure, that

NEW HAVEN, FROM FERRY HILL.
From an old engraving.

in either of these places, if you sigh for a crowd, you may go to New York in three hours. If you sigh for the wilderness, the White Mountains and the Adirondacks are not much farther away.

I was at New Haven on the second centennial of the beginning of the college. It was a good time to see the matchless loyalty of the different classes as they made *rendezvous* in their old home. Wherever you meet these men it is interesting to see how they really think that there is no other university in the world than theirs. They have a fine quotation from something in an original document which says that the college is created "for the bringing up of men who may be of service to the state."[1] I was pleased the other day, when, in trying to find out something about their Governor Hopkins, one of the patrons of Harvard College while there was yet no Yale College, I found the same expression. He died in 1659 in London, and in his will endowed some New England academies and gave to Harvard College the money with which to this hour she gives the "Deturs" every year to deserving pupils. Worthy remark, is it not, that the money which he left, which was distributed to the legatees about the time of the Treaty of Utrecht, now yields one hundred per cent annually for the uses of this trust? Remember this, ye gentlemen of Con-

[1] Cromwell, in giving counsel for the education of his sons, speaks of service to the state as one of the purposes to be kept in mind.

Yale College and State House, New Haven, Connecticut.
From an old steel engraving.

necticut who live at home at ease, when you send down for your friend to ride up from his office, and make your will. Men die, but universities, they have a good chance to live. There are many Hopkinses in America. I wish that some one of them would tell me where our Governor Edward Hopkins was born — not in Shrewsbury, as Cotton Mather said he was. Was it in Ecton?

It was thirty years ago that one of the most distinguished graduates of Yale College said to me that it had a great advantage over other institutions because it pleased the Lord God always to send into the world exactly the right person to be president at precisely the time when he was needed. This prophecy of his has been confirmed as the generation has gone by.

I was about to say that I had two grandfathers in Yale College in the seventies of the eighteenth century. Nathan Hale, whose statue looks out on Broadway, was not my grandfather. He never had any children, but he was the brother of my grandfather Enoch Hale, and they were together in college. Nathan Hale was only a little more than a year younger than my grandfather. I

LYMAN BEECHER.

have the letter in which their father, Richard Hale, told them that their mother had made cloth enough for their winter clothes and one of them might ride over to Coventry to be measured for both. Nathan Hale took a leading part in the "Beggar's Opera" when his society acted it before the college government of that day. The tradition says that his notes for that mysterious visit to New York which ended his life were written in Latin, and that he had appeared in New York as a Connecticut schoolmaster.

My children have a great many more Yale ancestors than I. Bright and wise men go to Hartford for their wives, and I followed that good example. So Lyman Beecher comes into our line, and so it is that the later Beechers, who did their duty so well a generation ago, are Connecticut born or bred. I do not remember if this story of Roxana Beecher has ever slipped into print. When she and her husband were young married people on Long Island, a member of the parish gave to her what I suppose was the Edinburgh Cyclopædia as a present. When the young family moved up into the mountains of Litchfield County, the cyclopædia went with them. When the first winter revealed to them the severities of that high altitude, Mrs. Beecher studied the pictures of Russian stoves in the cyclopædia and constructed the first of such comforts for the parsonage. As I write these words I remember that John Pierpont, the poet, who moved from Litchfield to Boston at about that time, invented a new stove which he put upon the market, and when the ecclesiastical council was called to determine whether

JOHN PIERPONT.

he had or had not done things which a minister should not do, the invention of this stove came in among the complaints of his enemies. Ministers ought not to invent stoves any more than they ought to write poems for theatres. Yet

I remember in later days Dr. Bushnell invented a furnace and no one took exception.

If you want to have a pleasant summer home and at the same time be within an easy ride of New York, you will not go wrong if you look up a house in that same Litchfield. The famous Gunnery is not far away. The wonderful waterfall at Bash Bish is not far away. I believe that is within the present line of New York. It was once in what they called Boston Corner and was part of Massachusetts. But as no Massachusetts sheriff could arrest a man in Boston Corner without having to carry him through New York or Connecticut as they went to the jail, Boston Corner

BASH BISH FALLS.

seemed likely to become a place without law, and we Massachusetts people gladly added it to the territory of New York, though we have not much territory to spare.

New England's first war, one is sorry to say, was in Connecticut, and the savage for the first

DESTRUCTION OF THE PEQUOTS.

time knew who his master was when the train-bands stormed the palisades at Mystic.

Old Dr. Dwight, President of Yale College, wrote the first guide-book of New England, and that is excellent reading to this day. I have spoken of it already. In early life, when he was in his poetical vein, he wrote "The Conquest of Canaan," and when Washington and the army were besieging Boston in 1775 and 1776 the Yale

Dr. Timothy Dwight.

College tutor came to camp and modestly asked the different gentlemen there to subscribe for the printing of his poem. My great-uncle, Nathan Hale, was there, a lieutenant on Winter Hill. He had told his men that they should have all his pay as bounties if they would enlist when their terms expired. But all the same he subscribed for "The Conquest of Canaan." Alas! before the book came to the press Hale was dead. Dear Dr. Dwight, as he was to be, wrote in these additional lines in memory of his pupil-patron: —

> "So, when fair Science strove in vain to save,
> Hale, doubly generous, found an early grave,"

and so on.

In the same poem, I forget how, Dr. Dwight brings in the Connecticut River. How it got into "The Conquest of Canaan" is not of much importance, but it is here that he says: —

> "No watery gleams through fairer valleys shine,
> Nor drinks the sea a lovelier stream than thine."

At that moment the only streams which he could have seen were the North River, the Pawtuxet

River, the Charles River, and possibly the Merrimac. But we will grant him a poet's privilege and even if we have seen a thousand other streams drunk up by the sea, we will stand by Dr. Dwight.

I am afraid that dear Dr. Dwight is more often spoken of now as the President of the college than as the leading poet of his time. But Connecticut people in particular and their descendants of two, three, and four generations ought not to forget his verses. As I go over the Railway to-day I am almost sorry to see that Stafford Springs is becoming a great manufacturing town. But the dear old hotel where the invalids of a century ago repaired in their own carriages with their own spans of horses and their own negro drivers is still extant, and, if you will ask at the right place, they will show you the sign-board which used to be displayed over the bath-house with this verse of Dr. Dwight's: —

"O health, thou dearest source of bliss to man,
I woo thee here, here at this far-famed Spring.
Oh, may I ere long welcome thy return!
Irradiate my countenance with thy beams,
And plant thy roses on my pallid cheeks!"

Scene in the Connecticut Valley Tobacco Fields.

To tell the whole truth, I never think of Dr. Dwight as the theologian encountering Voltaire and Volney in the lists of battle, but as a dear old poet with the roses of Stafford Springs beaming on his cheeks once pallid.

As they are finding radio-activity in mineral springs just now, will not some one ride over from Hartford and see how much there is at Stafford?

Samuel Taylor Maynard, the accomplished creator of the school of agriculture at Amherst, said to me once that whenever Massachusetts wanted to raise her own breadstuffs, she could do it in the valley of the Connecticut; and I do not dare say how much leaf tobacco the valley of the Connecticut will send to the market this year — the best, I believe, that the market will have to offer.

It is to us people who live in Massachusetts Bay an interesting thing to see that from the very beginning we have depended on the West for our bread. "Give us this day our daily bread, Good God, and we will send for it wherever Thou shalt require." Our first Governor, John

Winthrop, had to send back to England for meal and corn by the very ships which brought him and his. They arrived in England in a time really of famine. But his friends executed his orders. They bought meal of different grades in the highest market of that day and despatched the relief ships as promptly as might be. In the *Lyon*, one of them, it is said there arrived a certain Robert Hale to whom this writer is much obliged, and a certain Roger Williams. The *Lyon* is the ship which came up the Bay when a Fast Day had been ordered by the Massachusetts Board of Assistants. She broke open her hatches — and the Board ordered the Fast Day changed to a Thanksgiving Day, the first Thanksgiving Day known in the Bay. That lesson was enough for Winthrop, and with that spring (1631) he sent the first trading shallops into this valley of the Connecticut to buy for us the grain which he would turn into meal for feeding his fifteen hundred people for the next year. And from that day to this day the Bay has bought its breadstuffs from the West. Just now I think an occasional car-load slips in from

California. I know that Ventura County in southern California supplies the baked beans for my Sunday morning breakfast.

Here, then, is the history of the Connecticut

SETTLERS OF CONNECTICUT

In 1636, Mr. Hooker & his Congregation (about 100 in number,) travelled through the Wilderness, and began the settlement of Hartford, Connt.

Valley. And to this valley as early as 1634 such men as Hopkins and Haynes and Hooker and the first pioneers of Hartford crossed the wilderness of Massachusetts. Three weeks the journey took, which I take when I choose in three hours.

I wish some of that bright set of people that they have in Hartford would take time enough in

THE CAPITOL AT HARTFORD.

winter to write us a good history of their "littery fellers," the circle of wit and learning and men of letters who lived in Hartford a hundred years ago. Why should not Professor McCook or Dr. Ferguson or dear Mr. Clemens or Arthur Perkins or his sister retire into their inner consciousness and go into Miss Hewins's charming inner room or rummage in the manuscripts of the alcoves of the Wadsworth and tell us more about those bright men who wrote such bright things between

THE DEATH OF CAPTAIN FERRER, OF THE "AMISTAD."
From a contemporary engraving.

1790 and 1820? That capital ballad, "Franklin one night, cold, freezing to the skin," was printed in the Hartford *Courant* of that time. Really, it would not be beneath the notice of the Hartford *Courant* to unveil to us some of the secrets of Connecticut literature a hundred years ago.

They are always having picturesque things turn up in Connecticut. There is not in history anything more dramatic than the story of the

Amistad which worked itself to the dénouement here. The *Amistad* was a slave ship. She had brought from Africa to Havana a cargo of negroes. At Havana some Spanish planter bought the cargo, pretty much as it stood, made perhaps some additions there, and they were to be carried in the *Amistad* to his plantation. The poor fellows had had enough of slave ships, and they rose on the Portuguese crew and turned the tables. The blacks were in command and the whites were the prisoners. Then where were they to go? Some divine inspiration, I do not know what, bade them steer north. They understood American politics better than Mr. Van Buren did who was the President at that time, and they knew that North meant freedom. So they sailed north and north and north till a revenue cutter stumbled upon them off Long Island and brought them into a Connecticut harbor.

Who says there is no Providence when he reads that Connecticut farmers received these poor waifs struggling to be free? Well, things were not then just what they are now. Mr.

Roger Sherman Baldwin.

Van Buren, a Northern man with Southern principles, was President. He hated to bid his Connecticut marshal set these people free. He did his very best to have them return to Cuba. Say what you like to-day about him and his, you have to account for that *Amistad* business somehow. But thanks to King Alfred and Runnymede, John Davenport, and Hooker here in Connecticut, we have something which is called habeas corpus, and so our *Amistad* negroes can sue out their habeas corpus in a Connecticut court, and so Martin Van Buren and the whole Southern crew will be put to trial. And Roger Sherman Baldwin — a good name for the business — and John Quincy Adams, a name as good, had to maintain the right of freedom in all the courts. And so at last it comes to Washington, and the crisis comes before the Supreme Court. Send over to the Public Library and get John Quincy Adams's diary, which tells the story of that trial. Adams had not appeared in court since he was a youngster. Now he had the freedom of fifty-three men to maintain, and he had a court half of whom had been appointed by such men as Van Buren and Jackson liked to put into it — Southern men with Southern principles. The morning comes of the day of decision, and as John Quincy Adams rises from his bed they bring him a newspaper which announces to him that the night before one of the leading Southern judges has died of apoplexy. In that death the balance of the court is changed, and the fifty-three black men were set free. Their children are freemen to-day in the valley of the Congo. Let one of my young friends who wants a theme for a tragedy try his hand on this story.

CHARLES GOODYEAR.

Do not tell me that what Mrs. Richmond says

John Quincy Adams.

From the painting by Edward D. Marchant, 1847, in the New York Historical Society.

of workshops does not admit of poetry or dramatic incident. Take such an invention as that of Goodyear's india-rubber, born, bred, and per-

ROGER SHERMAN.

fected here in Connecticut. Find somebody to tell you the story of the growth of that mustard-seed into comfort for the whole earth, so that the Norwegian girl who is picking her way across a peat bog at the head of a fjord would bless Mr. Goodyear and his wife and his children if she knew to whom she owed her dry feet of that morning.

General Putnam.
From the painting by Wilkinson.

Go over to Salisbury and wake up some of the memories of the times when they stamped our first copper cents, or when Knox bade them cast cannon and they did so. They say dear Roger

Sherman was a shoemaker. I do not know, but I do know that every central suggestion in the American Constitution, "the wisest work of men's hands that was ever struck off in so short

General Putnam's Feat at Horse Neck.
From an old engraving.

a time," is the suggestion of this shoemaker, Roger Sherman.

There is a kind of promptness about these people which comes out in the most charming way in history. As it happened, and I have always been glad of it, I was in the room with Grant when somebody told him a story how, six months before Lexington, General Gage seized a powder-house of ours in sight of Beacon Hill, and how the news ran like wildfire down into Connecticut, and how, without any order from any Gov-

PUTNAM'S WOLF DEN.

ernor, the freemen of the town in which Grant's grandfather lived marched to the relief of Boston, and how his grandfather was among them. That is the sort of story which you can pick up any day in any town, if you will go to the right person and if you care about the realities of history.

John Howard Hale's Glastonbury Orchards.

Take Pomfret and Israel Putnam. What boy does not remember the wolf's den? Pomfret is well known now by hundreds of people who find it a pleasant summer home, as well as by other hundreds who live there. The cave in which Israel Putnam killed the wolf is still a cave where a wolf could be killed if a man with a gun entered behind him. And who is there of imaginative turn who will be much distressed if it prove that a hundred and fifty years have somewhat exaggerated the perils of the position?

Why one of the early Hales went to Connecticut I do not know. All I do know is that in 1634 people whose name begins with H — Haynes, Hopkins, and Hooker — went over and established Hartford; and now I know that if you go to Glastonbury you will be glad to make a visit to the great peach plantation of Howard Hale, whose peaches one or two hundred thousand of my readers have eaten since last June.

In the Civil War we had in New England a little company of men who were, so to speak, the "literary bureau" of the time. I could set type and was son of an editor, so it was my good fortune to sit in their councils, and another person who sat in their councils was a man named Ralph Waldo Emerson. Well! pretty much every Connecticut man who was worth his salt was off with Hawley (observe H again) and the rest lugging a musket around Florida or somewhere else among our old masters. So the political canvass in Connecticut of that summer devolved on old gentlemen who were too old to lug muskets. And so it was that the literary bureau had its part to play, and so it was that Ralph Waldo Emerson wrote two little tracts for that canvass. One of them is a very good picture of what we gain in daily life because there is no custom-house at the frontier of every state. Look among your old pamphlets, my dear cousins, and find that tract without the author's name. It is by the "Buddha of the West," the "New England Plato."

CHAPTER VIII

NEW YORK

This series of papers began in the counsels of Mr. and Mrs. Gentle Reader. As it happens, they end in the same counsels.

At that house they go to bed at 9.30. It was now five minutes before nine. He had just been reading to her Mr. Hale's paper about Connecticut in *The Outlook*. She said, "The trouble about Mr. Hale is that he always supposes that other people can do what he does. He has been at the top of Katahdin and at the top of Mount Washington and at the top of Mansfield and at the top of Wachusett. He has been on Ingham Peak in Rhode Island and on West Rock in Connecticut, and so he writes as if I had been there or as if we could go there as easily as we can go to bed."

"Well," said Mr. Reader in reply, "I do not see why he should not say so. You and I are younger than he is, and we have this very summer before us. What do you want to do most?"

She said that she should forget everything that she had been told about New England, and that

she wanted something like what her old schoolmistress called a "review." She would like to take that review, and at the same time she would like to see something in her tarry at home travels which had not been described or represented in *The Outlook*.

"Very good," said he. "Mr. Hale begins by saying that New England is a peninsula with an isthmus not two miles wide at its western point.

LANDING OF HENDRIK HUDSON.

How should you like to go round by Bar Harbor and the end of Nova Scotia, see the Bells at Baddeck, and then go down to the Gulf of St. Lawrence, and make a call at one of Grenfell's hospitals at Newfoundland, take the steamer up to Montreal, and then go by rail to St. John's above the Lake;

there meet Ransom with our house-boat, and so go by the house-boat near Burgoyne's line to Saratoga? You shall arrive at Saratoga on the day of the anniversary of the battle of Bennington. I, meanwhile, will have my canoe painted. The day you start I will start, and I will go down the Connecticut and then paddle along the Sound from Saybrook to New York and put the canoe on the deck of the steamer which shall take me to Albany. Then I will paddle up to Cohoes and make a carry at the falls there, and so, on the sixteenth of August, I will get on the house-boat and I will find you all there. And at the spot where General Gates received General Burgoyne's sword, I will fold you in my arms and kiss you, and after that you will remember that New England is a peninsula and that you and I have stood on the neck which connects it with the mainland."

These words were spoken in their bungalow near Windsor in Vermont on the Connecticut River.

To all she agreed. Now you must know that they were at the omnipotent age. This age is any age between fourteen and ninety-five, if only you be pure of mind, peaceable, and easy to be entreated. For then you can use omnipotent power if you want to. In this particular case these young people had been married twelve years. He did not drink, nor smoke, nor play at poker or other games of chance. He had no yacht, and he disliked the stock market. She loved him and her children. Her French and German were better than his. They lived in the open air every moment when they could escape "those prisons which we call homes." So they were always a little beforehand. He was always surprised that his bank balance was a few hundred dollars better than he thought it would be. She was constantly finding that her dividends from the Green Consolidated were larger than she expected they would be. On this occasion they parted from each other for nearly three weeks' time — the longest parting they had ever known. He told Ransom to have the house-boat well scoured out, painted where the paint was worn; he gave him the money to buy two mules with, told him he was to have the house-boat at Whitehall on the sixth of August. She told old Ruah,[1] who had had charge of the children ever since Nathan was born, that she was to put the children on the house-boat at

COHOES FALLS.

Albany, and that Ransom would take them all to St. John's. Then she wrote Gertrude Ingham, the same who had been her literature teacher at Vassar College, and asked her to make the voyage to Nova Scotia, Baddeck, Newfoundland, and the St. Lawrence with her. Gertrude

[1] Ruah is short for Lo-ru hamah.

said she would come up to Windsor and join her.

Meanwhile, Mr. Reader had done as he said. He had given orders to John Tintoretto, the Italian who presided over such things up the river, to paint the canoe; he had sent down to Cocknell's for three paddles — one long one and two short ones. He had provisioned the canoe for a short voyage down the Connecticut River and through the Sound, and on the fatal Monday which the gods provided, they started on their way. You see, when they had this talk of which you have heard, at nine o'clock in the evening, it was about the time when the days were the longest. Before July was well advanced all these preparations had been made of which you have been told.

So she went to White River Junction, and they rattled across the country to Portland, with their *Outlooks* in their hands. They refreshed the memory of Maine and New Hampshire as well as you can from an express train. They went to Bar Harbor by the "Flying Yankee." They did not miss one connection at the New Brunswick

St. John, or at Halifax, or at Baddeck. At Baddeck they saw some of Mr. Bell's wonderful kites at Le Bras d'Or, which is the name of that great shore loch where a bath is so charming. By means known to residents of that region,

LAKE GEORGE.
The Narrows, with Black Mountain and Bolton, and the Hummock in the foreground.

they went across to the Newfoundland St. John's and then by great good luck they joined Miss Merciful as she was taking round some supplies to a hospital in Anticosti. Fortune favors the brave, and the *Strathcona* came along, and carried them from that ship to another on the north side of the river, and then there was a Government steamer to go that very afternoon up the St. Lawrence to Quebec, and of course it happened that Dr. Abernethy was on board, to whom Dr. Grenfell had given them a letter.

When you are at Quebec, everything is easy sailing to Montreal. I do not know which of these young women is the better traveller. I know they always light on their feet. They always see whatever there is to be seen, and it does not surprise me, therefore, that on the appointed day and hour, as old Ransom stood on the front of the house-boat, scolding and advising and keeping an eye on all the children and instructing dear old Ruah on the points where she was doubtful, Gertrude and Abra looked out each from her own window of the cab which took them from the Prince Royal at Whitehall down to the canal. Great was the joy, as you may imagine. The children had been more than a fortnight parted from their mother. Ransom had nothing but success to announce. Dear old Ruah, with worthy pride, said she had not had to give anybody any medicine, and that they had been good children all of them. Abra and Gertrude went round to see the mules, patted them and praised them. Without so much as turning the boat around, the mules were taken round on the tow-path and attached to the other end of the boat. The cabman was paid, with a shilling extra to buy candy for his babies, and before they were ten minutes older the reunited party were going south on the Champlain Canal, where the children had but just now, under Ransom's auspices, been travelling to the north. So they found the way ready for them, and so the mules, well pleased, led them step by step from "blue Champlain." Old Ransom sometimes, when they were coming to a lock, let the boy Nathan run along with him on the shore, finding wild roses and pond lilies for his mother.

Meanwhile, at Windsor, Mr. Reader had taken his own coat-box in his hand out to the express-office, had given his instructions at the post-office, where he found Tintoretto, and walked down

ALBANY.

From an engraving made about 1840.

to the river, rolled up his duster and tucked it under the front seat of the canoe, had bidden Timothy good-by, and pulled out into the Connecticut.

"1905," he said to himself; "it was in 1774 that John Ledyard floated down here from Dresden College, as he would have called Dartmouth College. That was the beginning of the Nile and Congo for him."

And for a little relief he stretched himself out in the boat, with one paddle in the water, keeping her head to the south if the river flowed south, and east when it flowed east, and west when it flowed west. There were places where he could run in under the shade, but not many such places now. There were one or two long reaches where he had to paddle if he meant to keep up a good average day's work. Sometimes at nightfall he padlocked the canoe to a convenient post and walked up into the town. He did this at Springfield, and at Hartford. But five times out of six he found some trees, where he could roll himself in a blanket and let the sun and morning birds waken him. At New York the day boat people were glad to take him and the *Water Witch* on board, and as the passengers came down he met the Birdsells and the Havilands and the

THE CAPITOL AT ALBANY.
From a photograph copyrighted by G. P. Hall & Son, N. Y., 1899.

Schuylers and a dozen other of the pleasantest people of the world, and they were early enough to pick out good front chairs on the upper deck, and so a very happy day was provided for.

At Albany he went up to see what was left of dear Hunt's picture of Anahita; he uncovered his head reverently before the noble statue of Robert Burns; he wondered how that man in the public

BATTLE OF SARATOGA. GENERAL ARNOLD WOUNDED IN THE ATTACK ON THE HESSIAN REDOUBT.

garden makes his lotuses and nymphæas grow so much better than Mr. Reader's do. He called on Mrs. McElroy, who told him good news, and an hour before nightfall he walked down to the landing to find that the *Water Witch* was ready for him. And then, under the strokes of his own paddle as he worked his way up the river, he should arrive quite on time to see the only house-boat on the Champlain Canal and to wave his handkerchief and to jump on board.

It is not part of this series of papers to give local directions to travellers, which they can obtain much more to their present point by the local guides and the local guide-books. Enough to say that he gave Abra the kisses which he had promised, that she did not refuse. Enough to say that he made the little boy ride with him from one of the streams which flows into the North River across to one of those which flows into Lake Champlain. Nathan is an intelligent little fellow who has lived in the open air, and was made to understand that this was the isthmus of the peninsula of New England.

They spent a whole day in going over the Burgoyne battle-grounds with a clever local guide, who had provided Baroness Riedesel's journal, and they read again her pathetic letters. He told them the story of the mysterious third Nathan Hale and perhaps mythical Nathan Hale. He made Nathan commit to memory, so that he could declaim it to his mother when they came home, the lines about the "great surrender," how the Brunswick colors

MADAME RIEDESEL.
From a portrait in her "Memoirs."

Gayly had circled half the world
Until they drooped, disgraced and furled,
That day the Hampshire line

Stood to its arms at dress parade,
Beneath the Stars and Stripes arrayed,
And Massachusetts Pine,
To see the great atonement made
By Riedesel and Burgoyne.

You see he tried to make the boy understand

GENERAL BURGOYNE.

that the battles at Saratoga are among Colonel Creasy's "Fifteen Decisive Battles of the World." The reader may go back in these papers to see what is said about this in the chapter on Vermont. Nathan, who understands a map, pointed out to him that the battles of Bennington were fought on the New York side of the Vermont line.

Possibly some enthusiastic German-American

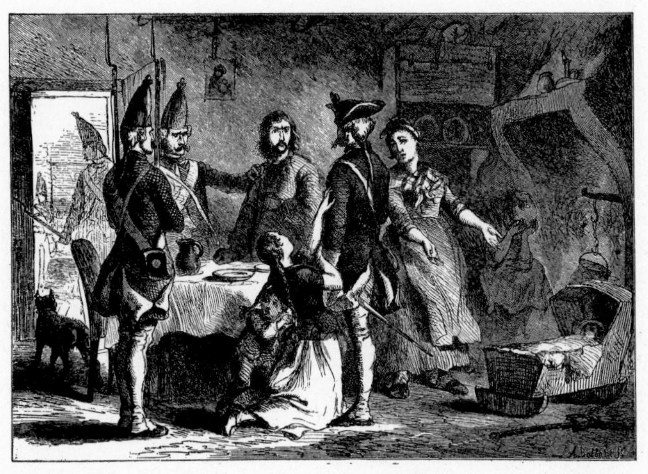

CONSCRIPTION OF GERMAN SOLDIERS FOR SERVICE IN AMERICA.

will write me a line to say just what the Brunswick colors and the Hessian colors were which were "furled" at Saratoga. We want replicas of those colors badly in the Old South Meeting-House in Boston, which is our museum of such things.

But somehow no one in Frankfurt seems eager to send them to us.

(In a parenthesis let me ask if you happen to know how the Rothschild fortune began. It was when one Napoleon was driving the Elector of Hesse out of his palace, and the Elector had some ready money by him. He found a young Jewish banker and placed his money in his hands at a very low rate of interest. It happened that the Jewish banker had no opportunity to return it till the Elector came back after a good many years, and on the profits on that silver money the Rothschild fortunes were already well begun. Now, if you please, that silver money which the Elector had in hand was the identical store of shillings and half-crowns which one George III. had paid this gentleman for the troops who were killed at Red Bank, who surrendered at Bennington and again at Saratoga, and who spent the rest of the war as prisoners of war in Virginia. Perhaps the House of Rothschild some day will be grateful enough for this acorn from which grew a great tree, to endow a university for the study of the metaphysics of war, in one of the Old Thirteen States. Saratoga would be a good place for it. There could be a long vacation in July and

BURGOYNE'S ARMY ON THE ROAD FROM LAKE CHAMPLAIN TO FORT EDWARD.

August, when visitors could reside in the college dormitories.)

No American will go to see the battle-grounds

of Saratoga or the place of the capitulation made by Burgoyne without remembering that, a hundred years after, a great American soldier died at Mount McGregor. Yes, and if any one wants to spend more time than our young friends did,

General Grant's Cottage at Mount McGregor.

here is the McGregor House, and hard by is Saratoga Springs, and not far away is Ballston.

I wish we could make room and had a right to print here the diary of Miss Edes, a pretty Boston girl who came to Ballston about a century ago with a great-uncle or somebody who was good to her; and she danced and perhaps joined in the flirtations of the infant watering-place. Recollect that "Ballston Spa" was a fashionable watering-place before Saratoga was. Ballston Spa,

BALLSTON SPA IN ITS FASHIONABLE DAYS (ABOUT 1835).

I think, is still the county seat. Not to go into geology or paleontology, for the present is more than we can handle, it will be enough to say that the different wells and springs both at Ballston and Saratoga to-day are what one may properly call bilge water of the early world. Fortunately for us of this time, the waters of that day settled in some sort of underground lake at the bottom, and so we are able now to drink water like what the megalosaurus or the Carnegiesaurus and other creatures of those early formations drank. People

VIEW OF SARATOGA JUST BEFORE THE MIDDLE OF THE LAST CENTURY.

who are old-fashioned enough to read the "Last of the Mohicans" and the "Pioneers" will find some nice allusions which Cooper made to the early outpour of the springs.

But Mr. and Mrs. Reader and the children had not time to study the geology or paleontology while they were in that region, and a day more saw them in their comfortable home, the house-boat, on their way to Niagara. They were quite careless whether the journey should last fifteen days or five-and-twenty days. In the open air, with God's sky overhead and all the time there is, and the good long days of August, and their own good company, with cardinal-flowers and pond-lilies, not to say an occasional sacred bean or water-chinquapin, there was enough to make a good large life of it, even if they did not pick up the morning newspaper.

Nine out of ten of the readers of these lines have no acquaintance with the house-boat but that which they got from Mr. Black's charming story of such a journey as this in England. But there are still left in America some of our old canals of the last century, where one can get away from cinders and smoke and dust, and have the comforts of his home and the joys of open-air life very closely knit in with each other. One of the very best of such opportunities is that given on the Erie Canal.

I have done my level best in the last few years to place the name of De Witt Clinton among the names of the American heroes in the New

De Witt Clinton.

York University. I am sorry to say that the New Yorkers themselves hardly seem to be aware that there was such a man; but all the same there was. De Witt Clinton, of the great house of

Clinton, one of the two great houses that fought each other in the early politics of the state of New York, was the leader of what was the Democratic party, which queerly enough in those days was called the Republican party. In 1801 he became senator of the United States. He left the Senate to be mayor of the city of New York, was removed and reappointed in 1811, and continued mayor till 1815. He took up early in life the policy of canal construction between the Hudson and Lake Erie and Lake Champlain. In 1817 a bill was passed authorizing the work at the expense of the State. In the same year he was chosen Governor, and in 1825 he had the "felicity of being borne from Buffalo to Albany in a barge, on the great work with which his name is identified."

With the construction of the Erie Canal the rapid development of the states then called the Northwestern states, which are now the great Middle states of the country, became possible. The success of that canal was an incentive in every American state to what used to be called "internal improvement." For these reasons I should have been glad if the honor, for it is an honor, of a place among the heroes of America in the Hall of Fame could have been awarded to De Witt Clinton.

The valley of the Mohawk gives a line so convenient that the suggestion of a canal was made

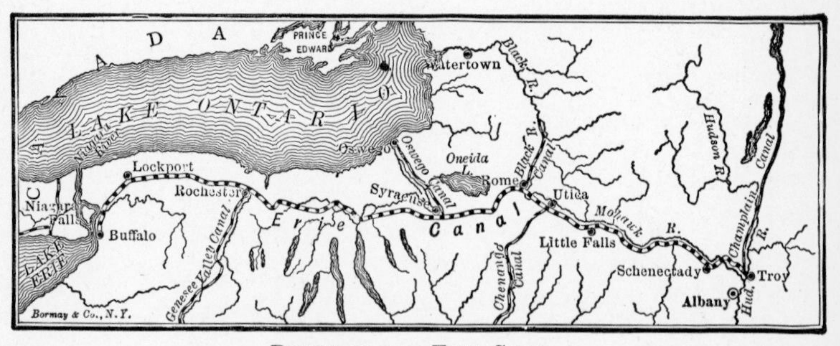

ROUTE OF THE ERIE CANAL.

very early. There is a story, undoubtedly authentic, of Washington, who knew from his boyhood the lake country to the west, predicting a canal here soon after the establishment of the Constitution. An attentive correspondent tells me that Washington invested money in the Mohawk Valley and that many farms near Little Falls are held under deeds from him. Between the

The Mohawk Valley.

Hudson River and the Lakes the highest summit which is surmounted by the lockage of the canal is 688 feet above the sea. The height of Lake Erie above the Hudson is 568 feet. The flow of the water eastward is calculated, I think, on a

View of the Erie Canal, at the Little Falls, Mohawk River.
From an engraving published in London in 1831.

plan of a moderate descent of half an inch in a mile. I believe the engineers to this hour think that the original construction reflected great honor on those self-taught engineers who were engaged in that work. They managed to build it for seven million dollars — an investment which has been repaid to the state again and again and yet again by the wealth, not to be calculated, which has made the city of New York what it is and the state of New York what it is.

Of course the cargoes which move from the West to the East on the canal-boats are much

ERIE CANAL, LOCKPORT.
From an early engraving.

more bulky than those which pass from the East to the West. A dollar's worth of grain takes much more room and weighs more than a dollar's worth of jackknives. Of course, also, it takes longer for a barge-load of grain to float from

Travelling by Packet Boat, Erie Canal.

Buffalo to Albany under the propulsion of some meditative mules than a car-load on a railway which travels by night as well as by day, with one of the giants of modern times leading the train. All the same, the transfer of the food of the West to the breakfast-tables of the East by the canal is very cheap, and the canal holds its own in face of railway competition. So you and I, dear Reader, if we live in a seaport, ought to be thankful for it, that it settles for us a good many of the questions as to the cost of freight.

This is certain, that whoever prays for his daily bread in the morning owes a good deal to De Witt Clinton and his followers, as the years go by. In December, 1815, a barrel of flour of the best brand cost anybody in Boston nine dollars. The best flour he can buy now costs five dollars and twenty-five cents. We owe the difference to the Erie Canal. One goes nowadays from Albany to Buffalo at the rate of fifty or sixty miles an hour. When the passenger service was well organized on the Erie Canal, the passenger boats went by day and night, and achieved eighty-five miles in twenty-four hours, on an average. But the traveller of to-day does not begin with Cohoes Falls. He does not see where Sam Patch made his celebrated leap, he certainly does not gather the sacred bean of India, nor does his little boy run along on the tow-path, and, if he capture a frog small enough, jump on board the boat with it and make mamma put it in her thimble. Such are the joys of such travellers as Mr. and Mrs. Gentle Reader. They do not, however, make eighty-five miles in the twenty-four hours, nor do they pretend to.

Dr. Eliphalet Nott.

Dear Innocents, they had all the time there is.

RED JACKET, SAGOYEWATHA.
From the painting by Robert W. Weir.

This is the phrase which Red Jacket used and which Mr. Emerson used to quote with so much humor. If anybody wants to know who Red Jacket was, he was an Iroquois Chief on the line of this same canal. And if anybody wants to know when he was, let him go ask my dear sister Julia Ward Howe, who told me that when she was six years old her mother introduced her to Red Jacket in his home. No, no, no! Abra and her husband were in no hurry, the children were in no hurry, nor were the mules in any hurry. From time to time old Ransom affected to be in a hurry, but really he was not in a hurry. I am painfully aware that this reader will not follow their example, but let us hope that he is not in such a hurry that he must cross the state in five hours, must "do" Niagara in five more, and must return to his brownstone house in New York by a night train.

Schenectady? Yes, of course they stopped in Schenectady. They had many pleasant people to see in Schenectady, they had to hear the traditions of Dr. Nott. It was vacation time, so that they could not see all the pleasant people, but

they could refresh themselves on the historical centres. They shed the right number of tears

Schenectady, from the West.

over the grave of Miss McCrea; they saw the Glen House or the Saunders House. Reader called it the Glen House and Abra called it the Saunders House. Here are their notes on Schenectady:—

"Have you not read up about the Schenectady massacre? It is high time you did. At all events, you will like to go down to the Saunders house, which stands as a sort of memorial to that massacre, although the house which now stands was built afterwards. This is the family of the Glen. Perhaps you do not know that Saunders and Glen are the same word. This family of the Glen, I say, were always good to the Indians. They always had something to eat for the Indian tramp, and they never fooled him by giving him water too hot to wash his hands with. They were nice to him. What happened then, when the massacre took place, was that the Glen family or the Saunders family — have it as you like, though nobody called them Saunders then — were spared, and their house, too, was not destroyed.

"Now, if any student of the higher criticism

wants to know why Saunders are sometimes Glens and Glens are sometimes Saunders, 'let him read,' as Mr. Browning says. Some of these people went down to Louisiana, and one of them, being named Alexander Saunders, used to be

GLENS FALLS.
From a photograph, copyrighted, 1890, by S. R. Stoddard, Glens Falls, N.Y.

called Sandy and Sanderson there, and was then called Saunders of the Glen. When his children and his children's children grew up and came back to Schenectady, some of them thought they were Saunders and some of them thought they were Glens, and they chose their names accordingly.

"It was exactly as Lafayette had six names he could call upon, and if he did not want to be Lafayette he could be Motier. But you can find the Saunders House if you want the Saunders House. If you want memorials of the Glen, you can go over to Glens Falls."

There are most charming bits of family history, Cavalier and Puritan, which the Saunders-Glen people of to-day have preserved. Central is the interesting story of the way in which the Saunders house was protected when the rest of Schenectady was swept by the barbarians.

As you go west as the Readers went, or on either of the railways, you can see the pretty "chutes" where the Indians said the sun rolled down as he was approaching his setting. For the benefit of the New York *Observer*, I will say that in literal fact the sun does not roll down this mountain side; but there are periods of the year near the month of June — trust me who have seen it — when the sun hugs the mountain range curiously close, and to the savages, who had not studied with Flamsteed, Langley, or Pickering, it did appear to roll down on that toboggan slide.

But it would never do to try to tell what they saw, nor will *The Outlook* care to publish their journal from one end to the other. One thing Mr. Gentle Reader learned which he had not learned before, though I had often told it to him

SALT MANUFACTURE AT SYRACUSE.
1. Solar Evaporation or Salt Fields. 3. Interior of Salt Blocks or Boiling Works.
2. Exterior of Salt Blocks. 4. State Pump House and Reservoir.

— he learned how this country is governed by its small cities and its large towns. He learned that in such places as Schenectady and Utica and Syracuse and Batavia and Rochester and Le Roy and Buffalo and a hundred others, the public opinion of the town is generally sound and strong, and that dawned upon him which I had not been able to impress upon him in talking — that a great city like New York or Philadelphia or Chicago or Boston has no such control over the real policy of the country as have, in the aggregate, such towns as Akron and Goshen and New Padua and Runnymede, which make the public opinion of Us the People. A man learns this lesson very well as he goes from one end of the state of New York to the other. In the Vermont chapter I spoke of a speech I made in the city of New York at a great Alpha Delta Phi convention. In that speech I called attention to the fact that a member of the lower house in Albany represents about as many people as a member of the English Parliament represents. Somebody in the audience laughed. I said: "I am sorry that any person laughs. The three persons whom I recollect as members of the legislature of New York would certainly have done honor to any parliamentary assembly in any nation in any period of history since parliamentary institutions took on their present form." The three people whom I had in mind when I spoke were Andrew Dixon White of Syracuse, Carleton Sprague of Buffalo, and Theodore Roosevelt of New York City. I think that twenty years have justified what I

STORMING OF STONEY POINT.
On the 15th of July 1779. Gen. Wayne with a body of American troops with unloaded muskets scaled the Fort at midnight and took the garrison (600 men) prisoners.

said of those three men. And I am apt to remember this speech of mine and these men when I read in a New York or Boston newspaper about hayseed legislation, with the implication that nobody knows anything unless he lives in the particular town in which the newspaper is printed.

When you go by canal or by the railway, you have a chance to see the oldest work of God which you will ever see on this planet, which I have referred to already in our first number. According to Agassiz and the other men who know, when this world passed into the Paleozoic out of the Eozoic condition — that is, when it passed from the dawn of life to the antiquity of life — certain red-hot rocks showed above the water, with much steam, I fancy, and much hissing. They were the range of ancient rock which divides the waters of the St. Lawrence from the waters of New England and New York. The railway as it runs west from Schenectady takes its course through this red rock, and Mr. and Mrs. Gentle Reader and the children saw it as the mules travelled along on the pathway of the canal. At Little Falls the boys rushed out to sell them diamonds. These are not of the brand of Golconda or Johannesburg, but they are cheaper, and the children were well pleased to begin their mineralogical cabinet with them.

No! I will not pretend to tell of the various adventures of those happy ten days. I will not tell of messengers up to cheerful-looking houses and the return of milk and cream and eggs for the support of man and woman. Then at such places as Ilion or Utica or Rome or Rochester, there would be a walk or a drive through the neighborhood, with every adventure ranging from the simplicity of a canal ride up to the highest civilization.

With the nice hearty inmates of other boats Reader and his wife and the children made cordial acquaintances, some of which will ripen into the friendships of half a century. For you must please to understand, dear reader, that the sailor, whom I must not call a seaman, who commands a vessel of three or four hundred tons which makes regular passages backward and forward from New York to Buffalo and perhaps farther west, lives on his craft with his family. The boat is their home. Nahum learns from his mother there that b-a-t spells bat, and Tryphena learns there how to broil a steak and how to bake a potato. If there were a long line of locks together, with so much of business as to keep the travellers half a day, our children played marbles with other boys of the fleet, or perhaps the girls from the rest of the fleet came aboard the house-boat and played checkers or backgammon.

Are you, alas! as fortunate as they in your vehicle? I am afraid you are riding at sixty miles an hour as you turn this leaf rather impatiently. But all the same there are one or two points which you should notice. Keep on the watch after you pass Schenectady if you are on the northern of the two parallel roads. Even to a flying traveller those black and red rocks seem more hard and cruel than most rocks do, and well they may.

They were what Charles Sprague saw, —

> "When the young sun revealed the glorious scene
> Where oceans gather
> And where fields grow green."

Certainly I do not know, and I do not think that anybody else knows, how long it was after the sudden uprising of these silent rocks before the ice-waves from the north, bringing down icy floes and glaciers even, came southward in their flow, lodged for a trifle of a few hundred thousand centuries (be the same more or less) on the north side of the Laurentian Range, and then surmounted it and all other such trifles, and passed southward till they melted away before summer suns. You and I need not bother ourselves about the length of time. What men know is that these waters which filled the Lake Ontario of that time, the ancestors of the waves which now go down the St. Lawrence so peacefully, were barred by the piles of icebergs in their way, and that they swept across to find the sea by way of the Hudson River. Men know their track by the boulders, and gravel-sheets, and bits of sand which they have left behind them.

When it was last proposed to enlarge the great Erie Canal, there were people who thought that this old tideway of the very dawn of things might be cleared from its rubbish and made to do our great business of daily bread. If you want to follow out this little bit of prehistoric annals, cross from Utica or Syracuse to Lake Ontario and find some of those intelligent gentlemen there who will give a happy month to you to show the course by which that unnamed river found its way to Manhattan and the sea.

Or, if you have not the month to give to this,

NIAGARA FALLS.

go down the bay between Staten Island and Long Island with some intelligent pilot, and he will tell you where is the deep gorge which those old icebergs chiselled out as they worked their way to the Atlantic.

Do not pretend to make your first or your fiftieth visit to Niagara without possessing and studying the directions to travellers prepared in 1903 by the Commission for the Preservation of Niagara.

In this very interesting report you will learn much that the average sightseer misses; you will learn things which nobody knew thirty years ago. One or more days may be spent to great advantage in following the Niagara by trolley, crossing it at its mouth at Kingston, and returning on the other side. Stop over at the station, where a very clever fellow (Yankee clever) will take you down into the gorge where Tom Moore thought how nice it would be

"By the side of yon sumach whose red berry dips
In the foam of this streamlet, how sweet to recline,
And to know that I sighed upon innocent lips
Which had never been sighed on by any but mine."

This is as good place as any to say that in any collected edition of Moore's poems the Gentle Reader will find a curious series of "Poems Relating to America." When Moore left Bermuda, "on account of a disorder in the chest," he landed at New York, and by what he called the "Cohos" came to Niagara, and so went down Lake Ontario and the St. Lawrence to Montreal, and Halifax, when he sailed in the frigate *Boston* for New York.

The poem from which I quoted four lines above is a very curious monument of the America of

FANNY KEMBLE.

that time. I suppose the *Boston*, which was an English frigate and not an American frigate, was the same *Boston* which the poor state of Massachusetts had lost to the English in the Penobscot in 1778.

It is quite worth while for any one who has a spark of historical interest to take with him on his house-boat, as he goes from Albany to Buffalo, the journal kept by the girl Fanny Kemble, as she went to the "Falls" for the first time. The journal ends at her first view of Niagara, "O God! who can describe that sight!!!"

There the reader can see how before the days of syndicates men travelled by rail. There was a superstition first that you had to have an inclined plane by which to ascend to a town or another by which you went out of it, as you ascended from Albany by an inclined plane. There was another superstition that when you arrived at a town you must leave the train and ride across in a different carriage (technically called a hack) to another railroad. Perhaps you went from Albany to Schenectady on one, from Schenectady to Utica on another, from Utica to Syracuse on another, from Syracuse to

Rochester on another, and from Rochester to Buffalo on another. One must not say it even in a whisper, but it required syndicates to unite these four or five roads into one.

If you will carefully read the Commissioners' direction for visiting Niagara, you will learn about the discussions which have gone on since Lyell's time, and even before, as to the place of the cataract in different ages, as to the different courses by which the waters from the upper lakes pass down through Ontario to the sea. It really seems probable that there was a time when the northern part of Lake Huron discharged itself to the sea by a much shorter channel.

Ah me! I have only brought our adventurous family to the western line of the state, and all southern New York is as yet in the inkstand.

The Outlook is so generous that it permits me to give my little boom to the Erie Canal, which sometimes seems to need a little cordial friendship in its various trials. But we cannot take the happy family back by the same route, for fear that they should be frozen up on the long level east of Rochester. The reader may take any route he chooses. There is the Erie Railway for instance.

Recollect, in general, O Gentle Reader, that

CHAUTAUQUA LAKE AND POINT.

New York is the Empire State because it holds this central place between the oldest mountains in the world and the latest Paris fashions as exhibited in New York stores. When you are by Chautauqua Lake, it is a toss of a sixpence whether your cigar end, when you throw it into a brook as you drive, shall go down the Mississippi and enlarge Florida, or shall go down the St. Lawrence, and feed the dun fish of your next winter's Sunday morning breakfast. Let me say in passing that if you have not spent a week at the annual Chautauqua you do not know your own country. There and in no other place known to me do you meet Baddeck and Newfoundland and Florida and Tiajuana at the same table; and there you are of one heart and one soul with the forty thousand people who will drift in and out there — people all of them who believe in God and in their country.

Farther east, whether you are on foot, as I hope you are, or are travelling in Mrs. Diederich Stuyvesant's automobile, as I hope you are not, you will be tempted by each of the Five Finger Lakes, as the geologists call them.

Here lived in happier days the "Five Nations," who became six nations. The Senecas, Onondagas, Mohawks, Cayugas, and Oneidas, to whom in after times were added the Tuscaroras. Here

Jemima Wilkinson settled among them, and introduced peaceful arts. Oh, that *The Outlook* would give me two numbers to tell who Jemima Wilkinson was, who is known to only one of the three million readers of this page.

If by accident any one wants to know how the

FALLS OF GENESEE RIVER, AT ROCHESTER.

Five Nations grew up to be one of the gardens of the world, let him read the new life of Jan Huidekoper. He will see here how a young Dutchman, landing when he was twenty years old with twenty dollars in his pocket, lived for six or seven decades and died in his own palace in Crawford

County in Pennsylvania, caring in the meantime for the Holland Purchase and for other like regions. The biography of one man serves you for a study of the history of a nation.

Rochester? Pray let us stay in Rochester for a day or two, if only to see the beauty of the fruit in August or September or October. Do you know that the Rochester Bank, which was the Flour Bank when Rochester flour was the best flour in the world, is now the Flower Bank, because the Rochester nurseries and gardens challenge the comparison of the world?

Syracuse? We must stop over here if it were only to see Mr. Calthrop and to go out to the model village where they make ready for market the alkalies which are far older than our Laurentian hills.

Utica? We shall have bad luck if we do not strike a convention there. And we must spend three or four years at Ithaca with Mr. White and President Schurman, and talk Browning with Professor Corson. We used to say of Ithaca that there were only young professors there, that they had their reputations to make and were making them. Now that they have made them, it is worth while to recollect that prophecy.

Among all these great names, which appear in every newspaper, I should like to remind the reader, who is very gentle, of what he never heard of, and that is Schoharie Cave. Back from the Catskills, back from Schenectady, back from Sharon, back from everywhere. It is one of those curious limestone caves in which the electric light now shows such wonders. And without going to the Mammoth Cave you may see here the underground wonders of the world.

JACOB GOULD SCHURMAN.
President of Cornell.

Sharon and Richfield and Saratoga and Ballston

and forty other watering-places all offer you their temptations.

The people of New York City themselves do not know the wonders of their systems of parks. I am sure I did not know them till a traveller

THE MALL, CENTRAL PARK.

from London, from the Park Commission there, told me how much time it had taken him to examine them, and gave me a hint of how much was before me when I had a month or two for the examination.

Fossils? Yes, fossils if you want them. Lions? Yes, lions if you want them. Here is the very lion which the little Carnegie girl saw in his cage somewhere on the Rhine and asked her father to send to New York. A great English botanist once told me that I could study palm-trees better in the great palm houses at Kew than if I were in Java or Malacca. I am quite sure that I know more of the habits of the hippopotamus from my observations in the Central Park than do all my bragging travelled friends who have been up the Nile and down half a dozen times.

The *Outlook* reader will be on the outlook as he tarries at home in his travels for something, be the same more or less, which will show him how man is to be lifted to the higher plane and come nearer to the good God. He will do well, then, if he take the *Outlook* office as a central point, and if, by the arts of a genial nature and the simple life, he communicate with the officers of the Associated Charities in the same building, he may learn from them more and more of the marvellous charity systems of the city and state.

INAUGURATION OF WASHINGTON.

Do not let Argus-eyed Press deceive you here. Argus-eyed Press has a knack of seeing the worst and making the most of it. If John Flaherty knock out his wife's brains with a flatiron, John Flaherty will be the hero of the next nine days. Meanwhile, hour by hour or day by day, week after week, assiduous, tender, Christian charity is working its way up hill and down dale in the great city and in the great state. At the office of the Associated Charities they will show the Gentle Reader how and where to learn what he wants to know of the care which men and women can give to men or women who are in trouble.

And in the organization of public education by steady steps, still advancing, the Empire State of New York has learned what it has to teach to the rest of the civilized states. Here at my side I have the last reports of the University of the State of New York — the One Hundred and Seventeenth Annual Report and the One Hundred and Eighteenth Annual Report. What is called the University of the City of New York is wholly different from that of the University of the State of New York. In the year 1784 the corporation of the Regents of the University of the State of New York was formed by the infant legislature. It is now a state department and at the same time a federation of more than nineteen hundred institutions of "secondary" and higher educa-

CONESTOGA WAGON.

tion. Its field includes high schools, union free schools, academies, colleges, universities, professional and technical schools, and also the work of education connected with the libraries, study clubs, and extension courses.

To speak of one detail of the supervision which this Board exercises over the higher studies, or home education department, the library department has been a model to the nation. It is difficult to make people understand that by the lending library system of the state of New York there are now in that state five hundred and twenty-one libraries, with two million three hundred thousand books, circulating annually on an average four hundred issues to each hundred families. The state established a library school which has attained a national reputation. The state Library ranks as second in the country in its equipment.

And so, Gentle Reader, we must part. We have travelled through seven states, and yet we have tarried at home. I did not know you by sight when we began, I do not know you by sight now. But then we were strangers to each other. Now I have that feeling of gratitude to you which none but he who feels it knows — none but a writer. He is used to readers who lay his valuable tractates down to be read on the next Sunday, and then to be forgotten with the dust of three days upon them. You have not treated me thus.

If you did, these words would be as blank paper to you.

Seven states we have gone through. They are states which have made their place in the civilization of the world and need not be afraid of their future. When in 1750 dear Ezra Stiles, who was quite competent to this duty, approached the history of one hundred and thirty years of New England, he ventured to prophesy. He had found out how often the population of New England doubled; he supposed that it would double three or four times at the same rate before another century ended in 1850. He was sure that the religion of the Con-

EZRA STILES.

gregational churches was the best in the world. He was sure that the stuff of which Connecticut and Massachusetts were made was the best in the world, and he calculated, therefore, that in 1850 six or seven million of us would be living in the

EMIGRATION TO THE WESTERN COUNTRY.

four New England colonies of his day, — well, let us own it, — that this confederated little nation would be as well advanced in the world as any of the old Englands or Hollands or France or Spain. He did not conceive it possible that any man in his senses would ever move west of the

Hudson River to live. Dear Ezra Stiles, I am afraid that he never pardoned his friend Franklin for establishing himself in Philadelphia.

It has not turned out just as Ezra Stiles meant it should, but when I go to Tiajuana, and when I spend a Sunday in Vienna, and when I take my coffee in the arbor in the Alhambra, and I run against a compatriot who has one of the New England names or those of their New York cousins, I am apt to find that he is glad to tell me that his forbears eight or nine generations ago came over with Brewster or Winthrop or Davenport or the Scotch-Irish or Knickerbocker or Stuyvesant. I do not find that those who come from the Empire State are ashamed of the Empire State, and I do find that those who have kinsmen in New England are glad that they have kinsmen there.

It has been a pleasure, Gentle Reader, to feel the touch of your hand and to wonder if one of your one hundred and twenty-eight ancestors who arrived in 1630 were, possibly, one of mine.

CHAPTER IX

WASHINGTON THEN AND NOW

WRITING in the city of Washington, which I first visited in 1844, I like to give some memories of that city, which I think I must have visited sixty-one different times since, before 1905.

The centennial of the city was observed with distinguished ceremonies by Congress in the year 1900. Mrs. President Adams's first drawing-room was New Year's Day, 1801. In a few words the history of the city's birth is this: By an act of 1790, the first Congress under the Constitution empowered the President to select a site for a "federal city" on the Potomac River. The "vote" was a very narrow one. The question of the site of the city had been the first geographical question which divided the national Congress. In the year 1861, when I paid one of my last visits to Josiah Quincy, he spoke of those debates and of the end of them by a vote of the Senate with the utmost bitterness. I had asked him, I think, when the North and South first measured swords. When he replied, I felt that he had a sort of contempt for my ignorance. He said it was on the question whether the federal city should be north or south of Mason and Dixon's line — that is, whether it should be in Northern or Southern territory. The balance between the twelve states was so even that the vote for a Southern federal city was gained only by the secession of a New Hampshire Senator, of whom Mr. Quincy spoke with the most bitter contempt, as if his vote had been treasonable. But the vote as given was given to the bank of the Potomac River, and

PRESIDENT WASHINGTON.

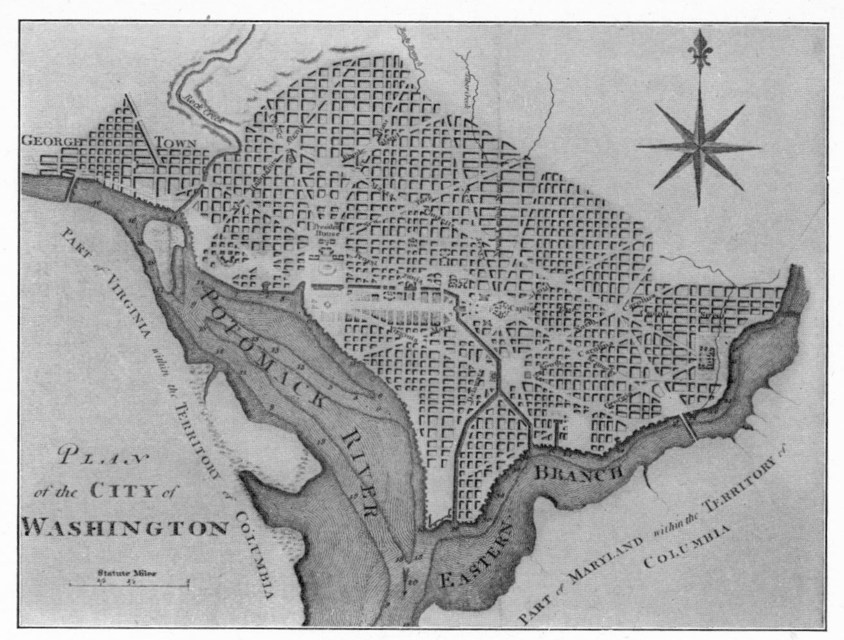

From an engraving published in London in 1798.

George Washington was directed to select the location.

In 1864, when I was on a visit to General Benjamin F. Butler at Fort Monroe, he called my attention to the rather curious fact that the site which Washington selected was the place where Daniel Defoe seventy-eight years before had put his hero Colonel Jack when he came to America as a white "apprentice." Colonel Jack, as this reader should know, was an English boy who had been kidnapped, as was the fashion in the time of Queen Anne and George the First, and so sent into the white slavery of Virginia. The history of Colonel Jack is to this hour the best narrative we have of the life of that class of men, the white slaves of Virginia at the end of the seventeenth century and the beginning of the eighteenth. The book is worth reading to-day because it contains Defoe's views of African slavery, and what ought to happen about it. And it is, I think, generally forgotten that the greatest hero of American literature, if we except Uncle Tom, is that man described by Defoe as being a

Brazilian slave-owner who was engaged in the slave trade when he was shipwrecked on an island at the mouth of the Orinoco. This slave-owner and slaveholder was Robinson Crusoe. In his memoirs, which have been more widely circulated than any book that was ever written excepting the Bible, there is never one expression of regret that he had engaged in the slave trade, or of reproof of the institution of slavery. But in Colonel Jack, Defoe does express himself as if it were desirable that that institution should come to an end.

It is interesting now to remember that a niece of his, named Elizabeth, left her friends in London and embarked for America. She was without friends and bargained with the captain of the ship to be sold on her arrival to reimburse the captain for her passage. Accordingly, that year, she was offered for sale in Philadelphia, and Andrew Job of Cecil County bought her for a term of years and brought her to his home. Such was the custom of that time. She not infrequently received letters from her uncle,

Daniel Defoe. From this lady came the distinguished family of Trimble, now resident, I think, in Maryland.

It requires a little vigor of the imagination to divine precisely the place of Colonel Jack's home. But he says himself, "It was our lot to be carried up a small river or creek which flows into the Potomac River about eight miles from the Great River." I think that General Butler thought that it said about eight miles from the Great Falls. As the story advances Colonel Jack was carried to another plantation larger than that where he worked before, so that the reader may imagine if he chooses, that he lived on Capitol Hill. Here he lived between five and six

MAJOR ANDREW ELLICOTT.

years. He then was established on three hundred acres of land.

Daniel Defoe had a son who emigrated to North Carolina, and I am told that descendants of that son may be living in North Carolina now. But the North Carolina people do not seem to know or to care. Is it worth while to say in passing that Oliver Goldsmith's trunk of clothes and of books went to Wilmington in North Carolina in the year 1722, that he never got them back again, and that possibly in some cellar in Wilmington to-day there might be found some poems of Goldsmith's which would be worthy the attention of *Harper's* or the *Century* or Mr. McClure?

To return to the city of Washington. It seems probable that George Washington selected Capitol Hill for the site of the Capitol of the new nation. It is the same hill on which three witches are represented in my own ballad as kindling the flame on the night of February 11 (22), 1732. But, for the benefit of the *New York Observer*, I will say that the existence of these witches is mythical. There is no evidence that they did not exist excepting in poetry, and there is no evidence that they did. All that is necessary to say is that, if they did, they were there about the time when Colonel Jack was on

VIEW OF THE POTOMAC AND THE SITE OF WASHINGTON IN 1800.

the same ground, and that they are persons quite as historical as he is.

The congressional battle over and the President having selected that site, Congress passed the necessary acts by which the District of Columbia was laid out, ten miles square, to be the home of the new city. When people growl to-day, as they do in the District here, that they are not allowed to govern themselves by universal suffrage, this is to be said, "Every one who has ever come here from the outside has come on that understanding." Thus, the Congress of 1790 had its eyes open and created a federal city with reasons which they thought good. The Congress of the Confederation had once and again been insulted by mobs in the city of Philadelphia. Parliament in London had been lately insulted by London mobs. In France the Paris mob had again and again shown that it could change the map of Europe, not to say of the world.

Whether right or wrong, the National Congress of 1790 meant to create a national city where the officers of the national government should not be exposed to the insults or the honors of a great city not under their own jurisdiction. They have certainly had their reward. Whatever the public opinion of the city of Washington is (and this would be very hard at any moment to tell), the city of Washington does not govern the United States as London governs England or as Paris governs France. And it ought to be remembered that it was established specially with the intention that it should not have any such political power. People who are interested in such subjects would do well to observe that most of the American states have followed this great example. That is to say, they have not chosen large

VIEW OF POTOMAC AND WASHINGTON EARLY IN THE LAST CENTURY.

cities for their capitals, but have intentionally placed them in small towns, perhaps in villages, where the local sentiment should be most inconsiderable.

The admirable adaptation of the spot must have presented itself to George Washington as soon as the plan was proposed. The very name of Georgetown for the city already standing there seems to show that somebody had already observed such fitness of things in naming this town from the king. I think that no other spot occurred to him, and I cannot find any reference to any in his correspondence or diary.

The organic act of July 16, 1790, placed the work of creation of the city solely in charge of President Washington, and it would seem that till his death he never lost the direction of the creation of the city. It seems certain that he directed Major L'Enfant, who laid it out on substantially such a plan as that which appears on the maps of to-day. There has been, and probably always will be, much discussion as to their real origin. L'Enfant was a young subaltern in the French army, who arrived with D'Estaing in 1778. He was wounded at Savannah, returned to France, and was engaged in the city of New York in reconstructing the building occupied there by the first Congress. He was afterwards in Philadelphia in the employ of Robert Morris, the financier. Morris's friends asserted that to L'Enfant's waste and incompetence Morris's financial ruin was due.

There is no doubt, however, that Major L'Enfant was employed by George Washington to draw the original plan of the "Federal City." But as early as January, 1791, Major Andrew Ellicott, who was at that time an officer of the government, was instructed by Washington to "go down to the spot staked out on the paper design." A letter from Jefferson, Secretary of State, dated January 15, 1791, says, "The President thinks it would be better that the outline at least of the city, and perhaps Georgetown, should be laid down in a plat of the territory. I have only now to send it and to desire that

CHARLES BULFINCH.

Major Ellicott may do it as soon as convenient, that it may be returned in time to be laid before the Congress." Ellicott was at this time in the government service, and the instructions to him, dated February 2, go into great detail. Money is furnished to Ellicott for the expedition, and we have a long letter from him of February 14, announcing the completion of the two first lines, with a letter to his wife. He writes again to her from Georgetown on the 20th of March, sending "a small bundle containing a pair of black silk mitts and a small smelling bottle which I hope you will receive as a small testimony of pure affection as ever had place in the human breast."

Here Ellicott worked all the summer. He speaks of L'Enfant as "my companion Major L'Enfant, who is pronounced in English Lonfong. He is a most worthy French gentleman." This is interesting because before November of that year Jefferson, who was Secretary of State, wrote: "It has been found impracticable to employ Major L'Enfant in the degree of subordination which was lawful and proper. So that L'Enfant had been notified that his services were at an end."

MONUMENT ERECTED IN 1860, AT THE NAVY YARD, WASHINGTON.

In 1802 a committee of Congress "find that the plan of the city was originally designed by Mr. L'Enfant, but that it was in many respects rejected by the President of the United States, and a plan drawn up by Mr. Ellicott which recognized the alterations made therein was engraved and published by the order of General Washington in 1792."

On the authority of this very strong statement in an official report, the friends of Major Ellicott have felt that full justice was not done to him when it was stated that the city as it now exists was the creation of L'Enfant. There is no doubt whatever that the city as it now exists follows lines of the surveys made when the region was almost a wilderness by Ellicott, and it seems to me equally sure that Ellicott was following as well as he could the general plan of L'Enfant, in which, however, he was privileged by his commission and by the necessities of the case to make frequent changes of detail. While, therefore, it is strictly true that the present city follows the lines laid down in the engraved plan of Andrew Ellicott, it is equally true that those lines were laid down in the wish to execute the general plan as it had been approved or used by George Washington and Major L'Enfant. Major Ellicott soon had a controversy with the commissioners as L'Enfant had done already.

In an interesting biography, published since this paper was originally written, Latrobe, a young Englishman, whose subsequent achievements like those of the rest of his family were those of Titans, comes in for a share of the credit in the original surveys of the city.

The L'Enfant plan is now well known to half the people of America, a very wise modification of what people call the "gridiron" plan, which, as I suppose, William Penn invented when he introduced it into Pennsylvania. By that plan one body of parallel streets run north and south,

BACK VIEW OF THE CAPITOL, WASHINGTON (ABOUT 1810).

one body run east and west. The Philadelphia people and most Western people like this plan, which is undoubtedly convenient for strangers. Boston people and people trained under the traditions of other centuries dislike it. The disadvantage is that you have little or no power of expressing your own wish when you go from one place to another, and that you may be in a very bad fix if, on a hot day in August, you are in Philadelphia and you have to walk two miles to the northward between quarter of twelve and quarter past twelve. You have no alternative: you must go with the sun shining on your back, and no emperor, pope, king, burgomaster, mayor, or chief of the police can help you. If you die of sunstroke before you arrive, your body will be decently carried to the morgue. But they cannot help you, they cannot prevent the sunstroke. Now, in a city laid out like Boston, where the streets follow the slopes of the hill or the curve of the shore, an intelligent person may elect by what route he shall go from one point to another, and how he may exempt himself from disagreeable contingencies, perhaps fatal contingencies. L'Enfant had the wit to adapt his city to both the systems. For the convenience of the mathematicians he laid out the gridiron city, where A B C D E F G, etc., represent the streets which run east and west; and one, two, three, four, five, six, seven, eight, etc., represent the streets which run north and south. But L'Enfant was a man of affairs — in a way he was a prophet — and he said to himself, "For what is this city built?" Answered by his good angel, "It is built to provide for the administration of a great nation." "What is the first requisition?" Answer, "That each department of the administration may communicate easily with every other."

MOUNT VERNON. THE TOMB OF WASHINGTON.

After receiving these inspirations, L'Enfant located on good places, as Nature had designed them, the points where the Capitol should be, where the Navy-Yard should be, where the Court-House should be, where the President's home should be, and where the Departments of State, of War, and of the Treasury should be. In those days the Navy Department was a part of the War Department. Men did not yet look for-

THE CAPITOL, ABOUT 1830.

ward to the Peace Department, as we do now, nor had the Patent Office nor the Post Office nor the Agricultural Department developed themselves. But, lest they should develop themselves, L'Enfant reserved squares or circles for them. Then on his plan he supposed that the President might wish to send his veto or his approval with the utmost speed to the Capitol, and so he drew in Pennsylvania Avenue from the President's house to the Capitol. He supposed that haste might be required from the Capitol to the Navy-Yard, and so he drew in an avenue there. In like manner he supposed that from each of his circles and squares to another people might wish to go directly, and he drew in avenues in other places. So is it that you have a double plan of "avenues" extending northeast, southeast, northwest, southwest, like the legs of a tarantula or other spider, making one plan; while the gridiron system, which is a system of so-called streets, makes another. This is the plan of to-day. Whoever writes the sequel to this paper in the year 1951 can explain what now exists in plaster in one of the rooms of the Library of Congress, the additions which hopeful people expect to make as this half-century goes on.

There seems to be no doubt that Washington and his commissioners, and L'Enfant as well, supposed that the principal residents of the city, with the single exception of the President, would fix their homes on the high plateau north and east of the Capitol. It is exactly suited for what the modern world calls the "residential" quarter of the city. Washington himself built his own house near the Capitol, just to the north of it, on this plateau. Pennsylvania Avenue, from

THE PRESIDENT'S HOUSE, 1832.

the infant Capitol to the infant White House, although running through what was very nearly a swamp, furnished cheaper lots. Naturally, as most business was done at the Capitol and at the White House, the most of what our native language calls "travel" went over that highway;

and tradition says that this is the reason why the city extended itself in that direction and did not take possession of what was meant to be the "residential" region. If you say this to a man from the Middle states or the West, he hardly

DEPARTMENT OF STATE. EARLY IN THE LAST CENTURY.

listens to you, he is so eager to say to you that all cities always grow to the west in America. This is rather a curious superstition which exists in this nation, built perhaps upon Berkeley's famous line, "Westward the star of empire takes its way." These things are what Western men say to you, as Herodotus says.

You will perhaps let me say in passing that my first acquaintance with that unknown land east of the Capitol, where the city of elegance was to have been, was formed when I was taken there in October, 1844, to attend the funeral of Adam

HOUSE OF REPRESENTATIVES, 1831.

Lindsey. This seemed so much like stepping into one of Scott's novels to bear my part there that I cannot help telling the story. In the days of the old French Revolution, when Robert Burns mixed himself up in French politics, and other-young Scotchmen with him, the Tory government of England pounced upon a lot of those young fellows and frightened them badly — I guess with reason. Among them was my Adam Lindsey, who fled to America, and here he thought he would be a market gardener in the new city, and he bought his land in those "residential" quarters. He was some four generations from the Adam Lindsey who befriended Mary Queen of Scots at Lochleven, and, so to speak, I shook hands with the old Adam Lindsey of many generations before. They told me, and believed, that the succession had been for all these generations in the same name.

In the last twenty years there has been no danger in sympathizing with Robert Burns's revolutionary views and hopes. But in his day Pitt's government was very severe on any expression of such opinions as his, whether in Scotland or in England. They followed up with bitter animosity Muir who had made a reputation among the extreme Radicals of England and Scotland, and they sent him to their new colony of Botany Bay. Another martyr of less degree was Fyshe Palmer, the Unitarian minister of Dundee. He also was sent to Botany Bay for seven years. At the end of seven years he was liberated, but before he returned to Scotland

VIEW OF WASHINGTON FROM THE CAPITOL, 1832.

he was shipwrecked on what is now our island of Guam, and there he died and was buried. But an American captain named Balch who was well up in democracy brought his body back to Boston to give it Christian burial. And here he was buried again in a public service conducted by

Buckminster. And if any antiquarian can tell me where his grave is, I will tell the people of Dundee who want to know, — not that they want to move the poor bones again, but by some proper tablet they would like to show that Fyshe Palmer's martyrdom is not wholly forgotten.

Robert Burns himself wrote one of his best odes in the days of the American Revolution. But at that time nobody dared print such treason. So it was only in 1872 that it was printed from the original manuscript. I have never seen it in any American Edition.

Every one feels the difficulty of remembering the mathematical and alphabetical names of streets. In 1844 a few of us devised a system of names for the streets, which have been waiting for sixty years for confirmation by the various governments of the city. A, B, C, D streets were to be Adams Street, Benton Street, Calhoun Street, Derne Street, and so we went on, till, at the end of the alphabet, you had Zebulon Street, in honor of Zebulon Montgomery. First Street, Second Street, Third Street, etc., were to be

Wonder Street, Tudor Street (in honor of the Virgin Queen), Trinity Street (for Trinity Church), Ivy Street (IV Street), Vermont Street, Virginia Street, Pleiades Street; Eighth Street was Atlantic Street, and then we had Muses Street, Tennessee Street, and so on. Poor Mr. McFar-

THE PRESIDENT'S HOUSE, FROM THE POTOMAC, 1839.

land, who, with his commissioners, rules the city so magnificently, will have to consider these names after sixty years, and, as he is apt to put things through, the calendar of such names will be well adjusted.

Washington is now a very agreeable city. It

is a very beautiful city. People who have nothing to do with the government of the nation like to come here to live. And no wonder. But for the tens and twenties and thirties of the last century, it is spoken of with great disrespect by the people who had to live there. To this day, when you go into the East Room at the White House with a guide who remembers the traditions, he tells you that Mrs. John Adams dried her clothes on washing day in the East Room. And the notices by travellers and the scraps which have escaped from old files of letters speak with great contempt of the infant city. The phrase "mud-hole" seems to have stuck, and certainly as late as the Civil War, before the wonder-works of "Boss" Shepard, it deserved that name. I remember seeing an artillery-wagon stuck in the mud in front of the Treasury Building, waiting for a relay of additional horses to be brought up to haul it out of its dilemma. A lady told me the other day that as a little girl she rode to Lincoln's second inauguration. The carriage stuck so deep in the mud that her father had to leave the carriage and assist in disinterring it.

The building of the city began after L'Enfant's plans and the work of the first generation which followed. As I am in the line of parentheses, I may say that L'Enfant, who as has been seen seems to have been a rather eccentric person, got into stiff quarrels with everybody else concerned, and retired to a plantation in the neighborhood, where his grave is still to be seen. The property was subsequently purchased by Mr. Riggs. Let us hope that before this Congress dissolves a proper memorial may be erected there to L'Enfant's memory. As for monument, he has a right to the inscription, "If you want a monument, look around."

I made my first visit to Washington sixty-one years ago, as I have said. I spent the months of October and November there, in a little brick house occupied by my dear friend George Jacob Abbot, the same who was afterwards Under-Secretary of State and United States Consul at Sheffield. George kept a school there, and he and I lived there together for two months, while the ladies of his family were at the North. In the rear of the house there was a little stable, and in that stable we kept our cow. The house stood where Mr. Pollock afterwards built a palace which is there to-day, at the corner of I and

WASHINGTON FROM THE WHITE HOUSE, ABOUT 1840.

Seventeenth streets. It was opposite General Macomb's house. For our one servant we had a dear old saint named Josephine Cupid, whose color may be guessed at from her name. The business of the housekeeping began when Josephine milked our cow in the morning, and then opened the stable door and drove her out to pasture. She came up by what would now be Connecticut Avenue to an open common, ten times as large as Boston Common is to-day, and there the cow spent her day with two or three hundred of her race and sex, eating such grass and drinking such water as a grateful nation and a good God provided. I doubt if the quantity of the food weighed heavily upon her stomach or her conscience. At all events, before night the memories of the stable came back to her, and half an hour before sunset she would be heard at the door. This means that in 1844 land was not of value sufficient north and west of that corner to be inclosed. Who owned it I do not know. Uncle Sam owned some circles and squares there. But the anecdote occurs to me because I have been writing the beginning of these memories in a closely built part of the town, quite in the heart of Josephine's cow's rampaging ground, which is to say, I suppose, about a mile from our stable. The city has grown, in those sixty years, from a mud-hole which had thirty thousand people, perhaps, within its borders, to a city of two hundred and fifty thousand inhabitants.

The only part of this common which was fenced in must have been near where the British Embassy is now. We called it the gymnasium, I think. That was the high-sounding name for a bowling-alley which the young men kept up. I remember one afternoon we persuaded Mrs. Madison, who was still alive, to visit us there, and with great effort she got a ball down the middle of the alley and was complimented on her knocking down the king. President Tyler came over and played with the young gentlemen sometimes. Everything had the simplicity and ease, if you please, of a small Virginia town. Whenever the weather would serve, a great many of the Southern members of the House or the Senate

MRS. MADISON.

rode to the Capitol on their saddle-horses. There were thirty or forty posts in front of the Capitol near where the statue of Washington now stands. You rode up to one of those posts and hitched your horse. You left him while you went in and attended the meeting of the House; you came

THE SMITHSONIAN INSTITUTE.
From an old engraving.

out and unhitched him and rode him to your two o'clock dinner.

I do not think that in the somewhat mechanical etiquette of Washington to-day we have improved on the familiar ease of social life in those days. If you were a youngster of five-and-twenty or thereabouts, you took your constitutional in an afternoon on foot or on horseback. Where shall we take tea? Let's go to Mrs. Seaton's; it's always pleasant there. So you rang the bell, which was immediately answered by a well-pleased negro; and you went into that large, cheery drawing-room to find perhaps five and twenty other gentlemen who had looked in at the same time. Somebody brought you a cup of tea, somebody brought you a biscuit. You stayed five minutes or an hour and a half, as you liked, and within ten days you looked in on Mrs. Seaton again.

I asked a friend in New England once what parallel we had to this in our New England cities, and he cried out, raising both hands, "Oh, if that happened once, your Mrs. Seaton would move out of town next day." Nor do I find anything quite like this in Washington in the arrangements of to-day, with Monday for Judges, Tuesday for the House, Wednesday for the Cabinet, Thursday for the Senate, and so on. One is a little apt to send his double to leave the cards in such a system.

For all that, one of the men most competent to speak in this world tells me that in no capital city of the world is "society so well organized" as it is here. Certainly I know no city where you can see so many agreeable people if you want to and if you have the time to do it. Washington people themselves say and think that in a year's time everybody in the world who is worth seeing

THE CAPITOL, ABOUT 1850.

looks in here. It is probable that this is a little as Abraham Lincoln said of a book, that people will read such and such a book who like to read that sort of book. The Washington people rate the social order of the world by considering first those people who have liked to come to Washington in the previous twelve months. Prince Henry, for instance, takes a higher grade in their book of notables than Prince Alfonso or Prince Karl. And it is true that agreeable travellers like to come here. It is true that the Ethnological Bureau has in its employ nine hundred accomplished men of science who have to be here once a year. It is true that the National Academy and the Colonial Dames and the King's Daughters and every other grand order in the country is apt to meet here, so that, whatever else you lack, you will not lack the society of agreeable people. About forty thousand New Englanders, as I count it, pass through Washington every winter southward because it is too cold in New England; while about twenty thousand other people of the same blood and lineage are going northward because it is too hot in Florida and Georgia. These people meet each other at Washington. The result is a little like that of putting cold water over an alcohol lamp when you want to make coffee. This winter has been especially cold here (the winter of 1905). They never had to shovel their sidewalks, I think. They certainly do not know how to do it, and in the middle of the winter the commissioner bade them put sawdust and ashes on the ice of their sidewalks, to the great surprise of a considerable part of the population.

To continue for a moment the comparison of the Washington of 1844 and that of 1904, I may

HOUSE OF REPRESENTATIVES, ABOUT 1850.

say this, that in square miles or square inches the nation of that day was not half as large as is the nation of to-day, and I may say that half the nation then was pretending and trying to feel a certain indifference toward national legislation, and I may say that everything then depended upon mails and nothing on the telegraph; and that the mail of that day took, on an average, five times as much time for its service as the mail does now. I remember seeing a man who had been riding day and night from New Orleans — "looked as if he had just come out of a state's prison," as somebody said. It was in Philadelphia, and he had been eight days and eight nights doing it.

So it happened that whoever came to Washington then felt in fact somewhat as a man feels who now happens in at Quebec or at Glasgow. He came out of America into Washington. Just now the truth is exactly the other way: you come into America when you come into Washington. Take my own dear townsmen. To this hour the very best of them doubt the real existence of any important communities in the world farther off than Springfield on the west, or Portland on the north, or Newport on the south. And those very people come here by stress of weather — a Raymond excursion party, for instance — somewhat as if they were going to the City of Mexico. They find here better houses than they left at home; they find the Congressional Library, they find people who have just happened over from Seattle or Santa Barbara; so really, for the first time, they get some idea of what their country is.

Indeed, one could not contrive a better little

NAVY YARD, WASHINGTON.

pattern of America than he gets when he goes through the street in which he passes a palace such as has no superior in the world and comes next to the clay bank left by "Boss" Shepard, next to which there is a slab shanty perched up on the top of a bank waiting for some Western Senator

THE GRAND REVIEW AT WASHINGTON. MAY 24, 1865.

to wish to build a palace there. I mean that the city is finished to the highest point of modern civilization in one place, and that it is left where L'Enfant and Washington left it in another. That makes an admirable type of the United States of to-day.

The winter of 1844–45 was the winter in which Texas was annexed to the United States. America cares nothing for history, and the generation of to-day does not even know by what ingenuity that annexation was effected. The Southern oligarchy of that time meant to have Texas as a part of the United States, let it cost what it might. Here was this fine region, as large as France, which had declared independence, and the Southern people wanted it because its position would turn the balance of slavery or freedom in the United States. For the same reason, the Northern people did not want it. It was then and there, for instance, that the state of New Hampshire, now one of the most strenuous of Republican states, turned right over from being the most strenuous of Democratic states. Under the leadership of such men as John Parker Hale, they refused to play the Southern game any longer.

A treaty had been arranged between the republic of Texas and the United States by which Texas should be admitted into our nation. As late as April, 1844, the Senate rejected this treaty by the vote of 35 to 16, while the treaty required two-thirds of the vote in its favor. So the magic of the "Joint Resolution" was tried. When you cannot do a thing by statute or treaty, you do it by a "Joint Resolution"; and the short session of 1844-45 was spent in driving through the two houses a "Joint Resolution" providing for the annexation of Texas.

This gave magnificent speaking in both houses. It witnessed the bolting of those Northern Democrats who then and there left the Southern alliance forever. And whoever lived in Washington thought it was the most important year in history.

I find a certain interest, therefore, in seeing that it now occupies fourteen lines in Bryant and Gay's History of five volumes. We Northern people

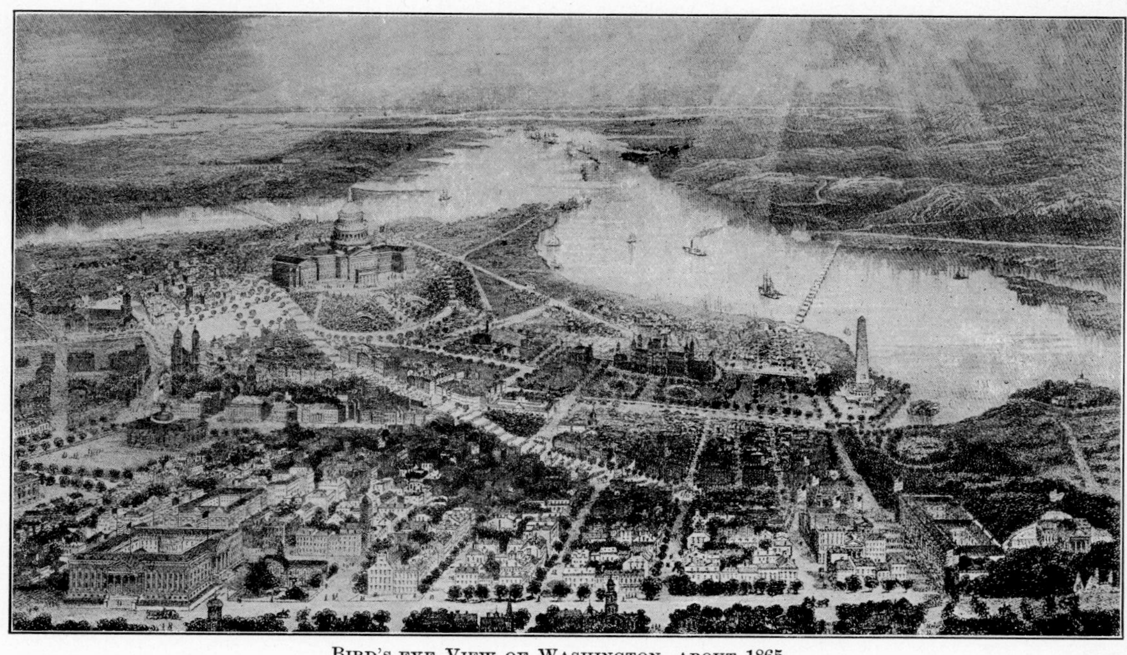

Bird's-eye View of Washington, about 1865.

had supposed that the Senate could be relied upon to defeat the Joint Resolution, though we knew the vote would be very narrow. But President Tyler was doing his best, and Mr. Polk's followers were doing their best to whip in recusants.

I left Washington, I believe, on the 3d of March, 1845. I know I was so angry at Polk's election that I would not stay to his inauguration. This was foolish in me. I called Mr. Rufus Choate, who was one of our Massachusetts Senators, out from the Senate Chamber and said to him, "I am going to Boston, Mr. Choate; what shall I tell my father?" "Tell him we are beaten, Mr. Hale. *Magno prœlio victi sumus.*" They had heard that morning that a certain Maryland Senator, about whose decision no one had known till then, was going to vote for annexation. When it proved a few days after that his son was appointed judge by President Tyler, people supposed they knew why that vote was given.

The constant pressure, one may say, of those great debates in the House and in the Senate interested the little city of thirty thousand people almost to a man or a woman in the proceedings at the Capitol. But as one sees Washington to-day, Washington cares very little what is going on at the Capitol. People are quite too dependent

WASHINGTON FROM ARLINGTON HEIGHTS, 1872.

on their newspapers to distress themselves. Exactly as there are many people in Albany this winter who have not been to the state Capitol of New York, as there have been as many people in Boston, Hartford, and Providence who have not been to the State Houses of Massachusetts, Connecticut, or Rhode Island, so you would find that in the city of Washington in the last winter two-thirds of the men and women had not been into the Senate Chamber of the nation or into the House of Representatives. But that was not so when the question in the Capitol was supposed to be the question whether the United States is a nation or the United States are a confederacy.

CHAPTER X

THE NEW WASHINGTON

YES, I suppose in a fashion all capitals are alike. But the people in Washington are a little apt to suppose that their capital is more like London or Berlin or Paris than it is. Napoleon used to say that there were men in cellars in Paris who had never heard of his name, who had never heard of Louis XVI's name, and who knew practically almost nothing of the years between Louis XVI and what Carlyle called the "whiff of grape-shot." I suppose something like this is true now. This could not be true in Washington. Yet in Washington there are thousands of people who are hard at work and do the Lord's business who are very indifferent to the names of the figureheads or the steersmen of the day. I have asked Cambridge undergraduates to tell me with whom they were reading their

Latin or their political history, and they have not known the name of their teacher. I do not think I could ask any official of the twenty-five thousand in Washington who was the President of the United States and find him ignorant. But I do think there is many an official in Washington whom I might ask to-day who would be Mr. Fairbanks's successor if the President and Vice-President died, and the man would not be able to tell me.

JOSEPH G. CANNON.

In every department, and this is fortunate for the country, there are some men quite too useful to be turned out on a change of administration. Whoever else goes, Mr. A. B. must remain, or Mr. X. Y., to keep the machine running. They told me in Paris when I was first there that when Louis Philippe became king, in 1830, there were clerks in the public offices who had served there since Louis XVI was on the throne. That was more than forty years. Directoire, First Consulate, Empire, Bourbon, it was all one to them; the king's work or the republic's work went on with even step, *œquo pede*.

Any change in such order, as you can see, is bad. I remember I once had a letter from Washington to ask me if I could tell them where Kohl's maps were — a collection of considerable value which Mr. J. G. Kohl had made for them. I said I would show them the first time I was in Washington, and then I took one of the gentlemen of the Department which wanted to know — took him in a cab to a house which the Department had occupied in the war, and went up into a particular hallway where was the original chest in which Kohl's maps were to be found. There have to be certain permanent people who remember such traditions of the Department.

Sometimes such people drop into the habits

of all chancelleries and adopt that infamous rule of feudal governments that it is better not to do a thing than to do it.

I love to tell the stories on the other side which show that with us the Sovereign is the People, that the Sovereign is in the saddle, and that the Sovereign pokes about in Washington as Haroun-

CONNECTICUT AVENUE, WASHINGTON.

al-Rashid did in Bagdad. The late Commodore Green told me that, coming home from the West Indies when he was a youngster, he said in the office of the chief of his bureau that he thought it was time that the longitudes should be readjusted by electric telegraph. If you will think of it, this gives you absolute precision, far greater than stellar observations can give. The chief of the bureau spoke of this to the Secretary of the Navy. The Secretary of the Navy sent the next morning for the young lieutenant, and at once asked him how he would take the longitudes, and, seeing that he had a head on his shoulders, gave him a small vessel for voyages in the Gulf of Mexico and all the men he wanted.

From this beginning began the system of telegraphic longitudes which has gone so far that now every hydrographic bureau in the world uses the longitudes which Uncle Sam has calculated from our own observations in every ocean. Green was at work in his little tent on an island far away, where they had a wire to London, when some English officers came in, introduced themselves, and were interested in seeing the processes. Green said: "Why don't you get some of this to do? The whole world is to be done, and you would like the work." To which one of them replied: "Get some of it to do! How should we get it?" "Why," said Green, "you would go to the Admiralty, tell them about it, and ask them to commission you." At which the Englishman replied, "Dear Mr. Green, if we spent half as

UPPER CONNECTICUT AVENUE, AND CORNER OF "OAK LAWN."

much time in the Admiralty as you have spent in talking to us, we should be kicked downstairs."

There is the difference between working in a country where the People is the fountain of honor and the Sovereign of the nation and another country where you have got to tell Quogga to tell Mingo to ask Sambo to ask Cæsar to send up your card to Mr. Smith to ask him to consult Mr. Jones as to whether Sir Stopford Buffles will appoint a day when he can receive you.

Two friends of mine, botanists, were coming up a few months ago from a botanical expedition in the South. They missed their connection in Washington, so that they had five or six hours to stay there. Without any introduction, they went at once to the Agricultural Department. There they were cordially welcomed by people who did not know their names, I suppose. They told of their interest in forests, they told just what they wanted to see and to know, and before they were five minutes older one of them was sitting by one cabinet in one room and another by the right cabinet in another room; and they had every facility for studying in the best collections of the world precisely the things which interested them and which they wanted to know.

Compare this with an experience of mine in London in 1859.

I arrived in London early in October. Mr. Bancroft, the historian, had asked me to make some copies for him in the State Paper Office. I wanted to do the right thing, so I called at once on the American minister, Mr. Dallas. Mr. Dallas will not mind it now if I say that he thought of himself quite as highly as he ought to think. He had a great respect for the letters of introduction which I brought him, and the whole interview was a fine illustration of etiquette, diplomacy, and red tape in which, dear reader, I assure you I could and can do as well as another if there is occasion. So I told him what Mr. Bancroft wanted and I. He said that if I would write him a note which he could send to the Foreign Secretary, the Foreign Secretary would send that note to the Home Secretary, and the Home Secretary would confer with the Keeper of the Records, and that he, Mr. Dallas, had no doubt that the Keeper of the Records would give me the permission I wanted. Here I, barbarian that I was, thanked him, but said if I might sit a moment at his desk I would write the memorandum; that

I wanted to see the portfolio of American papers, very limited, as I need not say, of 1584. Mr. Dallas's hair turned gray as I spoke of sitting at his desk. He said he thought I had better give more thought to the letter and had better

DEPARTMENT OF AGRICULTURE.

go to my lodgings and write him a note which, as before, he could send to, etc., etc., etc. I accepted the snub, went to my "lodgings," wrote the note, and have never seen Mr. Dallas from that day to this. What happened was this — that that evening I met at a little party Mr. Gardiner, the diligent and celebrated historian of that time, that the next morning he introduced me to Sir Francis Palgrave, the Keeper of the Records, that he gave me a line which opened the whole history of England for a thousand years to me. I made my copies and sent them to Mr. Bancroft, I suppose the next day, and then went off for ninety days on the Continent and elsewhere. On my return home in the first week of the next January, as I shook hands with the captain of the *Europa* in Queenstown Harbor, he said to me that I should find a note from the Foreign Office in my stateroom. I wondered what the Foreign Office had to do with me, and I ran downstairs to find a permit from the Record Office, countersigned by the Home Office, countersigned again by the Foreign Office, permitting me to examine the letters of the year 1584.

Now I do not say but there is more or less of this fuss and feathers in Washington, but I do say that when the People is Sovereign and the Sovereign is in the saddle, there is much less of it than there is where they are trying to maintain the forms of the Middle Ages and to use the machinery of Egbert or Alfred or William the Conqueror. This sometimes ends in putting Wamba the son of Witless, son of an alderman the son of a fool, into the cab of a modern locomotive to take an express train across the country.

There is an old saw, concocted a generation ago, which said that when a Boston man is introduced to a newcomer he asks, "What does he know?" That in New York the Knickerbocker asks, "How much is he worth?" In Philadelphia the people ask, "Who was his grandfather?" In which joke there is an element of truth. The Washington people now say that they ask, "What can he do?" I think that to a very perceptible extent this epigram is true.

The interesting thing about social life here is that you meet so many different sorts of people. You would not be surprised much if one of them had three arms, or if another had wings, or if another had some sort of ears or eyes which represented a seventh or an eighth sense. By this

I mean that the habits of one man have been so unlike those of another that you are somewhat surprised that you find yourself talking English with them all. They do not know it themselves,

STATE, WAR, AND NAVY BUILDING.

but they really live a good deal each man in his own world.

I said above that in the old days everybody in Washington kept the run of the proceedings in Congress, but now those people keep the run of the proceedings in Congress whose business it is to know what the proceedings in Congress are. But you shake hands with a press reporter and go up into the office of the "How To Do It Bureau," to find a gentleman who has not thought of Congress for a week. He probably knows that Mr. Cannon is the Speaker of the House, he is quite sure that he has heard of Mr. Gorman and Mr. Lodge in the Senate. But he dismisses them because they are doing their business; he is doing his. Well, it is a little as I once had in the same week a letter from James Haverstock in Burnside's army to ask me if I could tell him where his brother John was; and I had another note from John Haverstock to ask me if I could tell him where James Haverstock was. I wrote to each of them that his brother was in the same brigade in North Carolina that he was in himself, and that if he would get a pass from the colonel he could go over and see him. James and John were both in their duty; they were serving God, as the Prayer-Book puts it, in the condition of life where he had appointed them.

And it is a little in the same way that the gentleman in the "How To Do It Bureau" knows that the leaders of the Senate and the House understand their business better than he does, and does not bother his head about them at all. On the other hand, Mr. Lodge and Mr. Cannon have had things of certain importance to do.

PATENT OFFICE.

They have gained that certain experience of life and so they really think that the man in the "How To Do It Bureau" knows more than they do about the handling of yellow fever and the irrigation of Arizona. And this is to say that they have arisen to that sublime height in which a man obeys the instructions which are given to the Thessalonians.

As I have intimated, there is another element in the Washington of to-day in which the city differs entirely from what I call irreverently the Virginia "mud-hole" of 1844. By exactly the same law which sends the geese and ducks from beyond the equator to Bird Rock in the Gulf of the St. Lawrence and then sends them back again, a flock quite as large of New Englanders and New Yorkers pass south every winter to Florida and Georgia and perhaps Mexico and then pass north again as the spring opens; earlier or later, as the counsels of men or women happen to prevail in the separate families of the migrators. Well, exactly as the geese and ducks and rice-birds have to stop sometimes to rest themselves in their flight, nine-tenths of the people from the North have to stop at Washington to give two or three days to inquiries as to the government of the country and how it is administered. They do not stop at Chester or Perryville or Baltimore, though the train stops at those places. But at Washington they stop and spend what Miss Ferrier calls the rest day, the dress day, and the press day. Then they go on. Those same birds do not stop when they come back, but the tenth part which did not stop when they went on stop when they return.

This constant renewal of life, all belonging, as you observe, to the immediate family of the Sovereign of the nation, gives a curious element, or bright spots of gold, if you please, to each day, such as I have never observed in any other place in which I have lived. It is a very interesting element. It does Washington a great deal of good and it does this American people a great deal of good. In proportion as they make a longer or shorter stay, for the rest of their lives they believe the newspapers less or more when they read about Washington, and are better or worse informed as to the real government of the nation.

To meet such featherless birds of passage, if you are of the temperament of the people who like that sort of thing, you will look in at the Arlington or the New Willard or the Driscoll or the Normandie or all of them every day and shake hands with Mrs. Vanderlip, to whom you gave her degree at Chautauqua in 1893, or with Mr. Champernoon, whose father was at school with

WHITE HOUSE.

you at the Latin School in 1833. They will tell you the last news from New Padua or Fort Fairfield, and you will tell them whether the Cabinet changes mean a quarrel or have been foreordained from centuries. If, while you are talking with one or two of them in the great common hall which is now a part of every hotel, there turns up a very bright and intelligent-looking fellow whom they do not know but whom you do know, and the conversation suddenly changes to Nansen's book or to the temperature of Wilkes's Land in the Antarctic, that is because this gentleman is a press correspondent. I like these gentlemen, and they have been promoted step by step in journalism till they occupy the most important post in the metropolitan journals. At the same time, I cannot but observe that their presence in any circle is apt to throw a restraint upon the conversation there. If it happens sometimes, occasionally let us grant, but still sometimes, that the metropolitan journal or the metropolitan correspondent does not voice the latest whisper of the Washington circles, it is because of a certain reticence which is natural enough when they are present.

Now, let us contrast all this with the old Washington. I was walking down town one morning in 1844 and I met Joseph Grinnell, who was a member of Congress from New Bedford. I joined him, and he told me the morning's news. Samuel Hoar had arrived from Charleston with his daugh-

Post Office.

ter, having been turned out of that city by a mob of gentlemen, who waited upon him and told him that if he did not leave Charleston with his daughter a mob of blackguards would compel him to do so. Samuel Hoar would have been as willing to die from a Charleston pistol as any man, but he rightly measured the position, and with his daughter took the steamboat for Wilmington, and came up to Washington. This was seventeen years before Sumter, but Grinnell knew that it was the beginning of the Civil War. Before the morning had passed I had written to the *Daily Advertiser* in Boston the news of this crisis, and in two or three days the letter arrived in Boston. It was printed in the next morning's *Advertiser*, and in a day more it was in New York. It was copied in the New York journals, and was the first news which those journals printed of a transaction which we now know was critical in the affairs of men. I do not think there was a professional newspaper correspondent in Washington in the year 1844. I do know of our correspondents in the *Boston Advertiser* office, that the letters were from Mr. Winthrop and Mr. Grinnell and Mr. Choate, all members of Congress who had no idea that the *Advertiser* would need other information than they could give it. In earlier years the letters which will be found there by careful historians are from Edward Everett, Rufus Choate, Robert Winthrop, Daniel Webster, Joseph Story, and one or other New England Representatives. The earliest letter from my brother is of the date of 1843. The gentlemen of the press will excuse me and will agree with me when I say that the physical necessity which now compels so many square inches of news a day, whether there be any news or not, has not improved the quality of the daily letters which, naturally enough, the local press of every city has to print every morning or evening.

There was no better sign of the times in those early days than one could see in any issue of the Charleston dailies. Observe that not one of them printed more than five hundred copies. How they lived Heaven knows. But they did have an impudent habit of omitting national news, as if it were only by accident that they had any concern with it. Exactly as the *Tribune* has no separate heading every day of the action of the Swiss government, so the *Charleston Courier* did not recognize what was going on at Washington, except as it would an incident of general information. If it were proposed to inspect steamboats on Southern rivers, they would copy the information as they would have copied a motion in the British Parliament on the importing of cotton.

This single illustration suggests that it may be well to put in words the central distinction between the Washington of 1844 and that of 1905. The motto of the *Madisonian*, I think the paper was named, which pretended to be the special organ of the general government in those early days, was in the words attributed to Jefferson, "The best government is that which governs least." I cannot fix the quotation, and the fact that the *Madisonian* said it was from Jefferson is no evidence that it was so. But when you remember that in John Adams's time, when the yellow fever was in Philadelphia, Adams went to Braintree and the other members of his little Cabinet to their respective homes, and one might say there was no general government practically for many months till the Philadelphia fright was over, you understand what happened before the People were really wonted to the idea of a nation. You get traces of the same thing when you find that Jefferson never alludes to cotton-gins or steamboats, and that as far down as Jackson's time there were plenty of men to say that Congress could not appropriate money for a national road to the West.

Now you remember, by contrast, quite enough instances of coy indifference to national duties in your visits at different departments to-day. Here is the Department of Agriculture; it sends its agents over the world. A man in Guatemala finds ants which will destroy the cotton weevil in Texas, a man in northern China collects and brings home peach-stones of a variety invaluable to America. But if you had proposed a Department of Agriculture in John Tyler's time, you would have been told that the Constitution gave no power for any such thing. Or you go to Dr. Harris at the Bureau of Education; he is in correspondence with all the states and all the territories right and left; he is sending or receiving information for the whole nation. As a little side amusement and play the Department of Education has changed the whole interior life of Alaska by introducing reindeer from Siberia. Now, to have proposed a Board of Education in 1840 would have been madness.

The Civil War changed all that. As I am fond of saying, the United States is a nation, while our Southern masters were then saying all the time the United States are a confederacy. They pretended, when the President made an official pronouncement, that he held just the same relation to the United States as the Queen of Holland now holds to the forty states which have consented to the Hague conventions. But nobody says this now. Sam Adams and Patrick Henry from their seats in any other world look with amazement though with satisfaction on a capital of a nation which extends from sea to sea. It is a nation which understands home rule as nobody else understands it. Yet at the same time it is a nation which is not afraid to pick up a pin or to launch a navy if the needs of the nation require. At this moment the Department of Agriculture is engaged in the irrigation of a million square miles, be the same more or less. If you ask them, as the British commander asked Ethan Allen, by what authority they are acting, the Department of Agriculture would say, as he said, that they are at work "in the name of God and the Continental Congress." They would not talk about state sovereignty or state supremacy. They would say, I hope, that a good many million people in the world are asking God for their daily bread, and it is the business, as He orders, of the Department of Agriculture, to enlarge the world's produce of daily bread. "Time works with us," they will say, "and in a few years we will give you farms which produce a hundred bushels to an acre where the cactus or the mesquite now struggle for their lives."

Yes, the agonies of the four years between the 15th of April, 1861, and the 3d of April, 1865, can never be fully told; but this is certain, that the God of history has already given us the compensation for such agonies, as in the forty years which have passed since He has made it certain to the eighty million people between the Atlantic and the Pacific that the United States is a nation.

In the second year of the Civil War, a distinguished English traveller said to me that it was all very well to keep on fighting, "but, of course, you know, there cannot be, you know, a nation extending from the Atlantic to the Pacific. There never has been such a nation and there never will be. You will have to arrange for four different nations to cover that territory." To whom I replied, with rage hardly concealed, "There never has been such a nation, but it is the will of God that there shall be, and you will see that that is what we are fighting for."

Now, precisely as Jerusalem was a city guided by the priesthood, even if the technical rule was in the hands of soldiers, as Lowell is a city of weavers and spinners, as New York is a city of tradesmen buying and selling, as Princeton is a city of students and teachers, so is Washington a city of men and women who are fed by the nation, who work for the nation, who live for the nation, and as the nation chooses. Granting that half of them have ties and memories which bind them, say, to Georgia or Minnesota or the state of Maine, or to other states; granting that some of them even go to vote in those states as a sort of gallant symbol of their birth and education, all this is but a trifle, because their life is a national life. Twenty-five thousand people is a large number when you remember that the population of the white, which is the ruling race in the city, all told, is not more than one hundred and thirty thousand. When we were schoolboys, we used to say with James Otis, "One-fifth are fighting men." I suppose we could say of Washington now that one-fifth of its white residents are in the direct service of Uncle Sam — of the government of the United States. Now, for the loyal love which these people bear to the Union, to the nation of which they are, by whom they were nursed, there was really nothing to compare in the Washington of 1844, if you left out perhaps the members of the

Cabinet. This man was a Virginian, that man was a Carolinian, and, sandwiched in with them, one in a dozen, was some Northern man with Southern principles, but who would have called himself a New Yorker or a Michigan man, while his own successors in office to-day would say gladly and proudly that they are Americans.

INDEX